TH**INQ** 7-9

Inquiry-based learning
in the intermediate classroom

Jennifer Watt   Heidi Fuller   Wendy Terro

Published in Canada by Wave Learning Solutions Inc.
617 Logan Ave.
Toronto, ON, Canada, M4K 3C2
email: contact@wavelearningsolutions.com
phone: 1-800-314-4644
website: www.wavelearningsolutions.com

Printed and bound in Canada

1 2 3 4 – 19 18 17 16

ISBN 978-0-99-500183-1

Library and Archives Canada Cataloguing in Publication
Watt, Jennifer, 1965–, author

THINQ 7-9 : inquiry-based learning in the intermediate classroom / Jennifer Watt, Heidi Fuller, Wendy Terro.

Includes bibliographical references and index.

ISBN 978-0-9950018-3-1 (softcover)

1. Inquiry-based learning. I. Fuller, Heidi, author II. Terro, Wendy, author III. Title.

LB1027.23.W38 2017   371.3   C2017-904943-7

Publisher: David Steele
Production editor: Laura Kim
Composition: Janette Thompson (Jansom)

CONTENTS

FOREWORD

James Britton once wrote that "being told is the opposite of finding out." Britton's quote captures the essence of inquiry-based learning. "Finding out" is about constructing new understandings, developing realizations and gaining additional insights. "Finding out" requires that learners formulate questions, explore ideas, reflect on experiences and self-assess what is known and what is unknown. When adolescents are active participants in the learning process, rather than passive recipients of information, knowledge is generated rather than consumed. When knowledge is generated it leads to deeper insights, greater transfer, increased efficacy and ownership in learning. When one "finds out," learning happens and real change is realized.

At the onset of my career as a grade 7 teacher, I saw the value in promoting inquiry-based learning but unfortunately, fumbled my way through it. In those first trials, when I provided opportunities for students to pose and explore questions that were of interest to them, it was clear that it piqued students' motivation and engagement. An inquiry approach to learning even seemed to spark the interest of the students whom I perceived to be the most difficult to reach. Since inquiry-based learning was closely aligned to my belief that people learn by constructing their own understanding and knowledge of the world, I was determined to make it work. However, I was unsure of how to manage the environment, best support the process and accurately assess students' understanding. I was also unsure about how to help students become skilled questioners

and make sense of what they were exploring, let alone help them to arrive at a place where they were generating new knowledge and offering innovative solutions.

It is an honour to write the foreword for the intermediate edition of *THINQ* because this resource provides a comprehensive guide to implementing inquiry-based learning in grades 7–9. This book is *exactly* what I needed when I first tried my hand at fostering classroom inquiry. Whether you are new to inquiry-based learning or you have experience in implementing inquiry into your practice, this book will help you in many ways. You will learn about the essential traits of inquiry, discipline-specific inquiry models and the role of the intermediate teacher in inquiry learning.

Intermediate students bring a wide range of strengths, interests, experiences, and values to the classroom. At this age, students are developing the ability to think more abstractly and in multidimensional ways. They need to find relevance in their learning and want to assume a role in designing their own learning experiences. In the adolescent years, it becomes increasingly important to consider their need for autonomy, voice and self-efficacy in support of their development. Educators who read *THINQ 7–9* will acquire the knowledge, skills and strategies to ensure that intermediate students' classroom experiences are self-directed, empowering and relevant. In addition, educators will be able to foster inquiry dispositions, which are necessary for success in today's world.

THINQ 7–9 also provides strategies and tools for documenting, assessing and responding to student learning needs along with ideas to build assessment partnerships with students. Activities that will help teachers create a "climate of wonder" and foster dispositions of inquiry are shared. In articulating ways to support inquiry-based learning and helping educators to reflect on their convictions and commitments, no stone is left unturned. This resource will help educators, who might identify with my early attempts at inquiry-based learning, gain the confidence and knowledge to enact it meaningfully in practice. In addition, it will help to confirm the rationale for educators who have experience in implementing inquiry in their intermediate classrooms, and help them to further develop their capacity and commitment to engage students in authentic, meaningful learning.

Jenni Donohoo
Provincial Literacy Lead, Ontario Ministry of Education
Author of *Collaborative Inquiry for Educators: A Facilitator's Guide to School Improvement* (2013), *The Transformative Power of Collaborative Inquiry: Realizing Change in Schools and Classrooms* (co-author Moses Velasco, 2016), and *Collective Efficacy: How Educators' Beliefs Impact Student Learning* (2017).

ABOUT THE AUTHORS

Wendy, Heidi and Jennifer

Jennifer Watt

Jennifer is a program coordinator for beginning teachers and their mentors at the Toronto District School Board. She has been a history, politics, social science and English teacher, and a consultant for over 27 years. Throughout her career, she has supported both new and experienced classroom teachers at all grades and subjects in thinking about how to share their knowledge, experience and practices to improve student learning. Jennifer has a Master's Degree focusing on the assessment of teacher practice. She is the author of several books and her most recent publications are *THINQ 4–6* (2016) and *IQ: A Practical Guide to Inquiry-based Learning*, Oxford University Press (2014).

Wendy Terro

Wendy is a principal within the Toronto District School Board. She has held roles as a math coach, student work study teacher and classroom teacher working with students and teachers across primary, junior and intermediate grades. Wendy has led

professional development across the province in the areas of inquiry, assessment, math, equity and mentoring, and has worked extensively with schools and teachers on collaborative inquiry. She has taught courses on pedagogical documentation and assessment and is an advocate for inquiry learning and student voice and choice.

Heidi Fuller

Heidi is a grade 7 and 8 teacher in the Toronto District School Board. She has been an associate teacher, chairperson, presenter, mentor, and Ministry of Education researcher for 17 years. Throughout her career, she has taught primary, junior and intermediate, with an emphasis on critical-thinking skills through inquiry-based learning. Heidi's work with teachers, student teachers and administrators has centered on using learning goals, success criteria, descriptive feedback and differentiated assessment. In her work with intermediate students, she emphasizes the importance of wondering, questioning and exploring one's interests.

ACKNOWLEDGEMENTS

Thank you to the incredibly bright, generous and curious educators who are engaged in professional inquiries and who freely share the resulting adventures. Thanks to my writing partners, Heidi and Wendy. They both have a great sense of humour combined with deep insight into intermediate learners and the daily challenges and rewards of teaching. Thanks to Jill and David for their clear vision and remarkable talent. To my entire loving family, thank you. Congratulations, Matt and Elisha. Emma, you are an amazing young woman. Barry, you're the best. Sean, you're on your way to culinary greatness.

Jennifer Watt

I'd like to thank my husband, Eric for his support, love and encouragement and always helping me find time to delve into my work. To my three amazing children, Raley, Myria and Ronin whose curiosity and wonder have always inspired me! A tremendous thank you to Jennifer and Heidi for being supportive partners through this process. What a team! Thanks to the amazing educators I've had the privilege of working with who shared with me their curiosity and passion for inquiry and supporting all students. And lastly to my late Grandpa Dumville who was the ultimate lifelong learner. Thank you for always being there, encouraging me in every adventure and believing I could do it.

Wendy Terro

I would like to thank my parents for encouraging me to pursue my interests and do what I love. I also want to thank my husband, Luis, and daughter, Dahlia, for their support during the writing of this book.

Heidi Fuller

About THINQ

Making inquiry-based learning a practical reality for every classroom!

An ever increasing number of educators are exploring the potential of inquiry-based pedagogies to build a bridge to teaching, learning and assessment in a digital age. They instinctively understand that asking questions and seeking answers is a natural way of being a learner in the world. However, translating this basic truth into daily instructional practice is no small thing. This is the focus of *THINQ* — to help make inquiry-based learning a practical reality for every classroom, teacher and student.

We are writing the *THINQ* professional learning series from a teacher perspective, with an empathetic and realistic appreciation of a teacher's daily challenges. *THINQ* is designed to help teachers see how, over time, they can realistically integrate more inquiry-based learning into the context of their own classrooms.

THINQ resources are designed to:

- encourage teachers to do more inquiry.
- explore the big ideas of inquiry in an accessible and reader-friendly way.
- make explicit what inquiry can look, feel and sound like.
- demonstrate how inquiry-based learning can be assessed and evaluated.
- pose deep questions for teacher self-reflection and discussion with colleagues.
- provide case studies that introduce practical strategies with contextual examples.
- address common teacher questions and misconceptions about inquiry.

THINQ emphasizes the big ideas that underpin inquiry-based learning regardless of grades and disciplines. We also apply them to the specific needs and characteristics of learners at different ages and developmental stages: *THINQ Kindergarten, THINQ 1–3* (Primary), *THINQ 4–6* (Junior) and *THINQ 7–9* (Intermediate). We recognize that school jurisdictions organize their schools and grade divisions differently, but all of us share the understanding that there are distinct developmental learning stages. So while "intermediate learner" may not be the designation for grades 7–9 in your system, we feel confident, based on our work with teachers, that the students, issues and challenges are the same.

Professional learning — a personal journey

We believe that transforming the daily assessment and instructional practice of teachers is the single most important consideration in transitioning the traditional education system to digital-age teaching and learning models. But because change is hard, it is only really achievable if and when educators, individually and in collaborative communities, believe passionately in its benefits. They must choose voluntarily (not through coercion or compliance) to take up the challenge to change classroom practice and school culture. This is what *THINQ* is all about — helping educators reflect upon and move forward along their individual professional learning path.

We believe that integrating more inquiry rests, in part, upon a deep **conviction** that inquiry-based learning is needed and a personal **commitment** to persist until classrooms and schools begin to operate differently. Building the **capacity** to implement more inquiry in the **context** of one's own classroom and school is only sustainable if positive outcomes are **confirmed** by evidence and shared with others. Margin prompts throughout this book use these five Cs to provoke reflection, individually or with your colleagues, about your journey into inquiry-based learning.

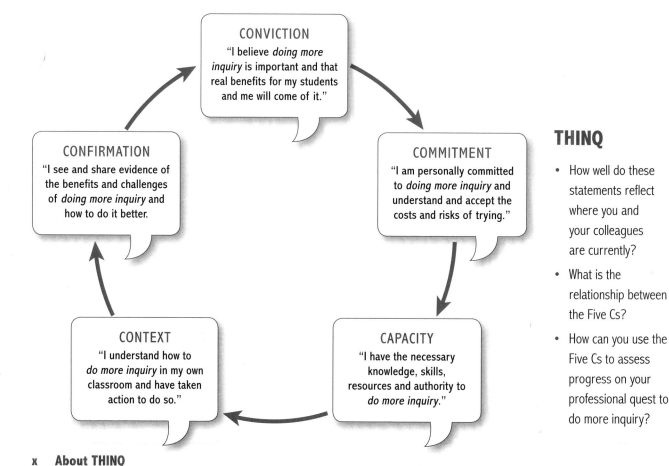

CONVICTION
"I believe *doing more inquiry* is important and that real benefits for my students and me will come of it."

COMMITMENT
"I am personally committed to *doing more inquiry* and understand and accept the costs and risks of trying."

CONFIRMATION
"I see and share evidence of the benefits and challenges of *doing more inquiry* and how to do it better."

CONTEXT
"I understand how to *do more inquiry* in my own classroom and have taken action to do so."

CAPACITY
"I have the necessary knowledge, skills, resources and authority to *do more inquiry*."

THINQ

- How well do these statements reflect where you and your colleagues are currently?

- What is the relationship between the Five Cs?

- How can you use the Five Cs to assess progress on your professional quest to do more inquiry?

Chapter 1
GETTING STARTED:
Inquiry-based learning with intermediate learners

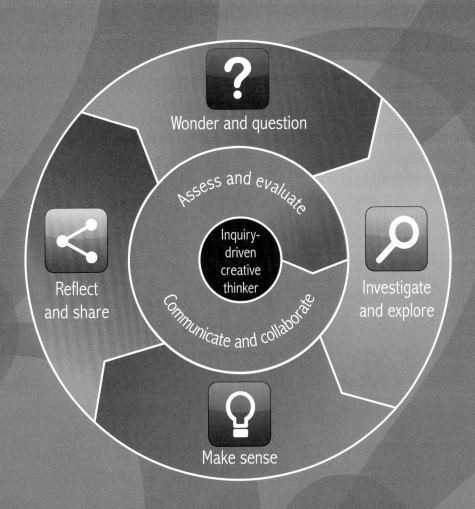

Wonder and question

Assess and evaluate

Inquiry-driven creative thinker

Communicate and collaborate

Reflect and share

Investigate and explore

Make sense

1.1 What is inquiry learning?

When we ask questions, wonder and formulate a problem, we are engaging in inquiry. It is rooted in our curiosity and desire to make sense of the world. It is a pedagogical practice that supports curiosity and wonder. Inquiry-based learning is not a new fad or method of teaching, but has been around for as long as educators have been interested in intellectual curiosity.

So why this resurgence in popularity? Inquiry-based learning offers an alternative to traditional learning where the emphasis is on the recall of facts. Students in this traditional style of learning tend to be passive participants, whereas inquiry learning teaches students how to learn and not just what to learn. As a form of deep learning, inquiry allows for integrating curriculum and results in less isolated and fragmented content.

Inquiry-based learning is an approach to teaching and learning where students' questions, thoughts and ideas are at the centre of the learning experience. For the learner, the process involves asking deep questions, investigating and exploring, engaging in evidence-based reasoning, and reflecting on and sharing the learning experience. For educators, the process involves being responsive to the learner's needs and knowing when and how to introduce ideas to move students along in their inquiry.

BIG IDEA

We learn by asking questions (inquiring) and are constantly creating new knowledge because knowledge is personally and socially constructed.

TEACHER VOICE

"If we want to create great thinkers, we have to give students opportunities to think. I have embraced inquiry-based learning in my practice because it requires students to behave as thinkers. It encourages them to do what good thinkers do: nurture their curiosity, read widely, make decisions, look for patterns and draw conclusions. It requires them to apply reading/ writing and oral language skills, rather than merely demonstrate an understanding of them.

Since the students 'own' every aspect of the inquiry process, their pride in their work, and in themselves as thinkers, is unmatched by any other pedagogical approach I have tried. They emerge engaged, empowered and aware that knowledge is something that is created, that shifts over time as new connections are made, as new information flows into the system, and that they could have a hand in contributing to that flow. I think it's this shift in thinking about thinking and learning that I like best about inquiry, the sense of students realizing that knowledge isn't fixed."

Claire Holland, Teacher

The essence of inquiry

Inquiry learning shares characteristics of many other pedagogies including constructivism, problem-based learning, active learning and social learning. The common trait among these pedagogies is the shared purpose of providing learners with opportunities to build knowledge. This collaborative construction and sharing of new knowledge provides momentum for future inquiry learning. Learning is not static, but constantly growing and changing based on the active participation of students and teachers within the learning experience.

CONVICTION
To what degree have you embraced inquiry-based learning in your practice?

Teachers should also be actively engaged in the learning and inquiry experience within the classroom. As educators, continually reflecting on what is working and how you can best support your students allows for your own professional growth. It is not expected that you know all of the content that your students will be exploring, but you should expect to be the activator of learning and provoke wonder in your students. While it can be overwhelming distinguishing inquiry learning from other pedagogies, it is helpful to remember what these pedagogies have in common: how knowledge is created, built and shared.

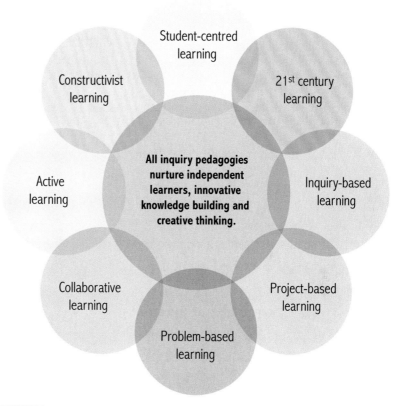

FIGURE 1.1 All inquiry-type pedagogies share a common purpose.

THINQ

- Did anything in the quote by Claire Holland resonate with you?
- What do you consider to be the essential traits of inquiry learning?
- What characteristics of inquiry learning align with your pedagogical approach?
- How important is it to have a common understanding of what inquiry-based learning is at your school?
- What are some strategies you could use to engage your colleagues in inquiry?

1.2 Why is inquiry a better way to learn?

Inquiry learning is rooted in educational and pedagogical philosophies that share the common purpose of developing students into independent learners, innovative knowledge-builders and creative thinkers. So what makes this a better way to learn? Central to inquiry learning is the promise of a learner-centred approach that allows students to explore the world, empowers them to seek answers, promotes creativity and develops ownership and purpose for learning.

Beliefs about learning

Understanding the historical place of inquiry in education allows us to appreciate its foundations as well as the tensions that exist between inquiry-based learning and more traditional approaches to education.

In the Socratic tradition, it was through questioning that the teacher and student would dialogue to find answers to questions that were worth thinking about deeply. This process pushed learning, clarifying basic assumptions and finding truth. Shifting ahead to the 20th century, John Dewey's thinking on education evolved the scope of inquiry to include the student's own experiences and building upon their prior knowledge. He believed that students should be actively engaged in the learning process and have a high degree of control over what they are learning. The teacher's role should be that of facilitator and the inquiry should be guided by empirical methods of creating knowledge. The purpose of education was to strengthen democracy, help students understand their full potential and to work towards a common good.

In contrast to Dewey's work were the prevailing views on education at the time, which was that knowledge was considered to be a collection of facts and procedures. Education was designed to meet the needs of an industrial society. Learners were seen as empty vessels to fill with facts and formulas, beginning with simple concepts first. Success was determined by how much students could recall. This linear process has been ingrained into our classrooms and education system and can still be heard echoing the halls of many institutions today.

BIG IDEA

Central to inquiry learning are beliefs about who learners are and what they are capable of.

CONVICTION

What are your beliefs about learning and learners?

FOOD FOR THOUGHT

"Every thinker puts some portion of an apparently stable world in peril and no one can wholly predict what will emerge in its place."

John Dewey

"Educating is always a vocation rooted in hopefulness. As teachers we believe that learning is possible, that nothing can keep an open mind from seeking after knowledge and finding a way to know."

bell hooks

"It is, in fact, nothing short of a miracle that the modern methods of instruction have not yet entirely strangled the holy curiosity out of inquiry.... It is a grave mistake to think that the enjoyment of seeing and searching can be promoted by means of coercion and a sense of duty."

Albert Einstein

Central to our beliefs about learning are our convictions about who learners are and what they are capable of. Inquiry learning is grounded in what we know, but also pushes us to ask questions to challenge our knowledge, looking at it from new viewpoints and perspectives. Inquiry learning encourages curiosity and places the learner in control. The learner is not passive but actively engaged in the process of learning, investigating real-world problems that are relevant to him or her. Inquiry learning changes the learner and the learning community within and outside of the classroom walls.

We have now reached our question of why inquiry learning is a better way to learn. Turning to research on inquiry will provide us with the benefits to inquiry-based learning. As highlighted by Colyer and Watt (*THINQ 4-6: Inquiry-based learning in the junior classroom*, 2016), the research work of Dr. Sharon Friesen and David Scott (Inquiry-Based Learning: A Review of the Research Literature, 2013) identified a wide body of research on the most common types of inquiry in North America. Some of the highlights of their research suggest:

- Inquiry-based approaches to learning positively impact students' ability to understand core concepts and procedures. Inquiry also creates a more engaging learning environment.

- Discipline-based approaches to inquiry learning (as opposed to minimally-guided instruction), if designed well, support students in deep learning.

- Disciplinary-based inquiry does not detract from traditional forms of assessment but actually increases achievement on standardized assessments (Friesen, 2010).

- Inquiry helps students develop critical thinking abilities and scientific reasoning, while developing a deeper understanding of science (Barrow, 2006).

- Problem-based learning increases student engagement in mathematics, a greater willingness to see mathematics as relevant to everyday life, and increases willingness to approach mathematical challenges with a positive attitude (Boaler, 1997).

- Problem-based learning fosters greater gains in conceptual understandings in science (Williams, Hemstreet, Liu and Smith, 1998).

CONVICTION
How convinced are you that research provides evidence of the benefits of inquiry learning? What other evidence would you like to see?

CONFIRMATION
Do your own classroom experiences confirm or contradict the research?

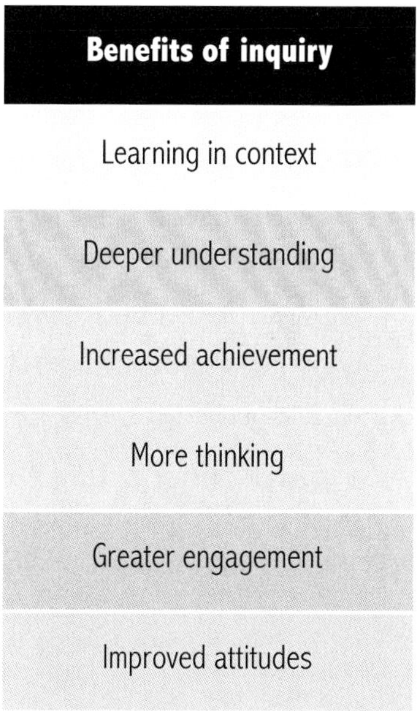

Benefits of inquiry

Learning in context

Deeper understanding

Increased achievement

More thinking

Greater engagement

Improved attitudes

FIGURE 1.2 Research indicates there are significant benefits to taking an inquiry stance to learning.

Teaching and learning in a digital world

Information and communication technologies are transforming our world. Today learners can easily access more information than they could ever hope to need or use. We have access to information where- and whenever we demand it.

Technology can support students in retrieving information, but it can also be used in ways that transform information, preparing students to excel in a knowledge-based society. Digital platforms allow students to collaborate with peers, share and exchange ideas and knowledge, and interact with experts. This changes the dynamic of the classroom from one where the teacher holds the knowledge, to one where teachers become an activator who supports students in digging deeper into topics that they are passionate about.

Traditional learning	Inquiry learning
Have to learn	Want to learn
What to know	How to know
Tell and memorize	Ask and inquire
Only one right answer	Many possible conclusions
Teacher directed	Learner centered
One-size-fits-all	Personalized
Passive learning	Active learning
Assessment for marks	Assessment for learning

FIGURE 1.3 By taking an inquiry stance, many important aspects of best-practice teaching, learning and assessment can be implemented.

This brave new world gives education a new purpose: fostering curiosity and asking rich questions; encouraging the use of intellect and curiosity to answer these questions; and providing opportunities for the sharing of new learning. Education today is no longer preparing students for one career but for multiple jobs in fields that have yet to be created. With the evolving nature of the 21st century, it will be less important for students to know specific information and more important for them to know how to get the required information and what to do with it in different contexts.

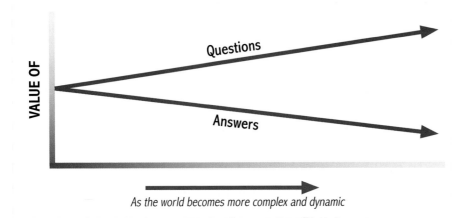

As the world becomes more complex and dynamic

FIGURE 1.4 In his book *A More Beautiful Question*, Warren Berger argues that in a more complex and dynamic world, questions become more valuable than answers.

Inquiry learning is good for everyone

Each learner is unique and our classrooms are filled with students with a complex array of strengths and needs. Inquiry learning provides opportunities for meeting the needs of all learners within our classrooms. Throughout the inquiry process, there is opportunity to work directly with students, assessing their progress and identifying areas in which they need more support. Students are actively engaged in the planning, development and process of their inquiry, giving them a deeper understanding of the learning outcome. Inquiry-based learning provides students with an access point to reach multiple areas of a curriculum; it also offers opportunities for students to develop important learning skills such as collaboration, responsibility and self-regulation. Here are some ideas to help support all students with inquiry-based learning:

- Identify prompts to help students decide what they want to learn.

- Share exemplars of previous inquiries with students.

- Know the whole student, including strengths, interests and learning needs to plan ahead and guide students when introducing new inquiry topics.

- Use your knowledge of your students' interests to support identifying an inquiry topic.

- Engage and collaborate with families and special education support teachers to maintain the direction of inquiry and make real-world connections.

THINQ

- Reflect on your own beliefs about learning. In what ways do they align with inquiry?

- In what ways would you have to change your role as a teacher by taking an inquiry stance?

- What additional support could you provide so all of your learners experience success with inquiry?

INQUIRY FOR ALL

Supporting all students

"The great thing about inquiry is that all my students are involved and experience success in their learning. I have a very diverse group of learners and I have worked with them to develop a strong community of learners who recognize their individual strengths and areas of need. They understand that we are all different and that difference contributes to a rich learning experience for all.

Good inquiry questions have personal significance and entry points for all learners. To support my students with special needs, I often focus on one or two inquiry skills (e.g., asking good questions, recognizing or developing reasons) and I also provide additional practice working with questions that have personal significance.

If I plan to support all my students, they can be successful in their inquiry. These are a few things I focus on:

- Developing a strong community of learners who recognize that we all have strengths and unique skills;
- Communication with parents to help make connections to daily life and build and deepen inquiry skills;
- Using technology throughout to support the inquiry process to develop questions, investigate, make sense and share their inquiry;
- Working with colleagues and special education staff to plan and help scaffold the inquiry;
- Being flexible and responsive to the needs of each learner; and
- Celebrating the growth of each student and sharing this with the learner, peers and families."

Lily is a grade 7 teacher who has been teaching through inquiry for a number of years.

1.3 What are inquiry dispositions?

Curiosity, critical thinking, open-mindedness and hopefulness in one's ability to reason are inquiry dispositions. These dispositions, as explored by Colyer and Watt in *THINQ 4-6: Inquiry-based learning in the junior classroom* (2016), help keep the learner on the journey of learning, support risk-taking and help them persist in the inquiry journey. They also help students accept failure as an important component of learning.

Creating an inquiry culture

Teachers should spend a considerable amount of time creating a classroom climate and culture that support the cognitive and affective domains of inquiry learning. With inquiry learning there is a shift in responsibility for learning that requires much more from the learner. This shift in balance can result in a range of emotions — from wonder and excitement to frustration. Building in time to check-in throughout the inquiry process will allow you to discuss these emotions and connect it to these inquiry dispositions. These check-ins will allow you to have discussions with students on what conditions are needed for inquiry learning and their contribution to a safe, respectful learning environment. This will happen with more frequency at the beginning of the year as the community is being established, and remain an integral component of inquiry learning to ensure students are successful in their inquiry process.

> **BIG IDEA**
> Inquiry dispositions support risk-taking and a sustainable commitment to inquiry learning

> **CONVICTION**
> How convinced are you that curiosity, criticality, hopefulness and open-mindedness are necessary conditions for learning?

> **COMMITMENT**
> When have you been most engaged as a learner and why?

Curiosity	**Criticality**	**Hopefulness**	**Open-mindedness**
Eagerness to learn or know something	Objective analysis and evaluation	Feeling or inspiring optimism about the future	Willingness to consider new ideas

FIGURE 1.5 Curiosity, criticality, hopefulness and open-mindedness are foundational building blocks for creating a sustainable culture of inquiry learning.

You have an incredible impact on developing these dispositions in students, and a great way to support this is through modelling these dispositions yourself. Share what you are curious about. What makes you wonder? What questions drive you? Your students will benefit from hearing of your experience as an inquiry learner. Sharing your life questions and journey will offer them an example of an inquiring mind and perspectives they may not have considered. Your enthusiasm will also demonstrate to them the excitement of asking questions, building knowledge and always being curious.

As with any pedagogy that requires students to take risks in their learning, there must be classroom conditions in place that support this. Getting to know your students, their identity, cultures and communities will provide the conditions needed for developing a classroom community that supports inquiry learning. When students feel they are a valued part of a community they are more likely to take risks in their learning, share their successes and challenges, and persevere in the face of challenge. On the next page you will find a table with suggestions on how inquiry dispositions can flourish in your classroom.

THINQ

- What inquiry dispositions do you possess? What do you need to continue exploring?
- What are some strategies you use to develop a classroom climate for inquiry dispositions?
- What strategies do you use to get to know your intermediate students?
- What actions could your school take to be more reflective of these inquiry dispositions?

TEACHER QUERIES

Are my students ready for inquiry?

This is a question we get regularly from teachers and the simple answer is — they are ready! We cannot wait until we think they are ready. Take the leap and begin engaging them through inquiry. There are conditions to learning that will make inquiry-based learning flow more smoothly and building a responsive learning environment is one of them. Here are just a few ways you can create a responsive learning environment:

- Incorporate collaborative learning activities into all areas of the curriculum.
- Design your physical space to promote collaboration and social interactions.
- Provide flexible work spaces for students to work individually or in groups.
- Make technology accessible to students.
- Have a visual space dedicated to curiosity — a Wonder Wall is a great way to provide space for student interests and inquiry questions.

Creating an environment that promotes positive social interactions and risk-taking requires the ongoing attention and involvement of students. Building a classroom community takes time and should be done with considerable emphasis at the beginning of the school year, and maintained throughout the entire school year.

Disposition	Description	Ways to promote the disposition in your classroom
Curiosity and wonder	You see the world as mysterious and have many questions and interests as you try to make sense of the world.	Create and share simple, open-ended yet purposeful provocations with your students to invite, entice and expand intellectual curiosity on a specific topic or concept. Common provocations include an interesting photo, book, picture, natural object, question, event, or an interest of the students. Create a wonder wall of student questions. Share your own curiosities, pivotal questions, interests, and the successes and pitfalls of your own inquiry endeavours.
Criticality (critical thinking)	You enjoy thinking deeply. This thinking may involve making predictions, verifying evidence and assessing arguments and claims. You do not accept arguments based purely on authority (because someone else said so) You like to figure things out for yourself. You take risks in thinking and accept that mistakes and errors are essential for learning.	Teach students and provide students with opportunities to: • construct and recognize valid arguments and conclusions. • recognize common mistakes (fallacies) in reasoning. • distinguish between evidence and interpretation of evidence. • continually reinforce that learning to think deeply is a challenge for everyone and that learning involves making mistakes (highlight your own mistakes to students and how you learn from them).
Hopefulness	You see the world as it is and like to think about how it can be improved. You do not accept the ways things are as inevitable. You care about and have a sense of purpose in your inquiries.	Inquiries involve problem-solving — they are future oriented. Do not deaden an inquiry process by presenting current knowledge as the be-all and end-all. Allow students to create their own knowledge and to be change agents. Recognize and model wonder about the world.
Open-mindedness	You are open to surprises. You consider many sides and perspectives when thinking. You are aware of your own biases and actively seek new questions and ideas about the world that you may not have considered before.	Highlight mysteries, big ideas and questions about the world. In preparing guided inquiries, be sure to provide evidence and arguments from multiple perspectives for students to consider. Provide multiple opportunities for students to self-reflect on their thinking. Tempt students out of their comfort zone by providing opportunities for them to learn more about themselves, their communities and the world. Have students create an "amazing and astonishing" wall that highlights new learning they have discovered through the inquiry process.

FIGURE 1.6 There are many ways to promote inquiry dispositions in your classroom.

1.4 Is there a standard model or method of inquiry?

In the previous section we looked at inquiry dispositions and why inquiry learning is the best way to learn. There are many pedagogies that encompass inquiry-based learning in their purpose and match it in quality. There are also specific types of inquiry that teachers can choose from. These include problem-based learning, project-based and play-based learning, to name a few. Your district or school may have a preferred type or you may begin by trying out a form of inquiry that relates most to your students' needs and interests.

There are many different versions of inquiry learning and it is easy to feel overwhelmed by the complexity of so many variations. Some focus on the creation and innovation of an object. Others focus on technology and the creation and sharing to a larger world audience. Some types are used with particular age groups. Regardless of the many types, we find it useful to focus on three essential traits that are present in all types of inquiry learning (Colyer and Watt, 2016).

Essential traits of inquiry

All inquiry is rooted in an essential question that invites the learner to wonder, think deeply and solve. Answering a question or solving a problem involves a method. This method involves discrete steps or stages of a cycle that help the learner with their thinking. This method may be particular to a discipline. In answering the question or solving the problem, the student experiences a developmentally-appropriate version of the way professional or expert learners in a field engage in their work. Like professionals, they think critically, self-reflect, contribute, communicate and share findings. New knowledge is created.

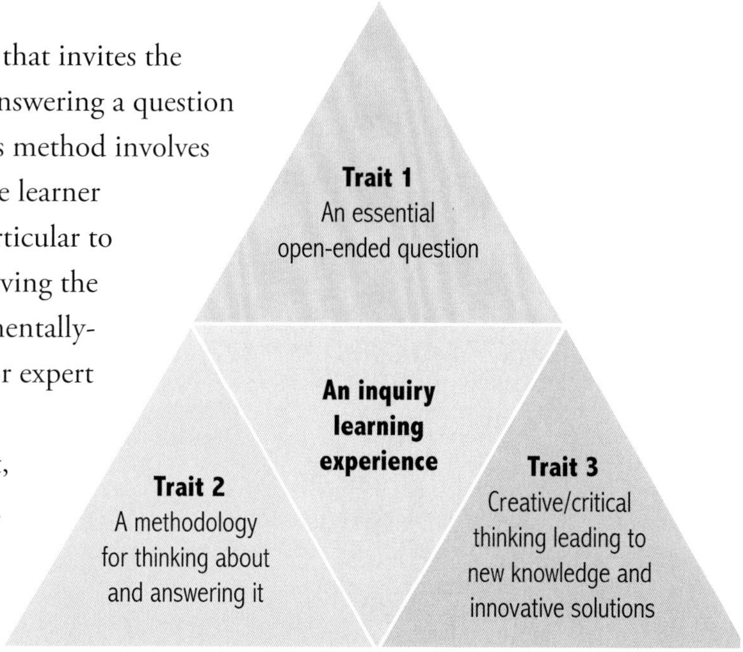

Trait 1
An essential open-ended question

An inquiry learning experience

Trait 2
A methodology for thinking about and answering it

Trait 3
Creative/critical thinking leading to new knowledge and innovative solutions

FIGURE 1.7 All inquiry learning experiences share three essential traits.

Discipline-specific inquiry models

Each discipline has its own way of building knowledge and identifying what it considers quality work. The inquiry process tends to follow the qualities outlined by the particular discipline. If you are doing a scientific inquiry, math inquiry or art inquiry, the method, steps, processes and questions of the inquiry can be distinct. For example, a scientific inquiry would focus on experiments and discovery whereas an art inquiry would be focused on the act of creation.

On the following pages, we have shared some flowcharts that represent the various inquiry models to help support students and teachers with the complexity of the inquiry process. Consider these models and how frequent referencing by the teacher and students would help address concerns and provide appropriate instructional support. The models of inquiry typically display the process in a linear fashion; however, do not be deceived by how they are represented. Inquiry is not a linear process but is responsive to the needs of the learner and can be recursive, flexible and loop back to a previous stage. This varies from the more traditional models of research that emphasized a lock-step approach.

While we advise not getting bogged down with one particular inquiry model, there may be spaces in which the intermediate teacher is subject-specific. In these cases, consider your curriculum documents as they may outline a specific inquiry model for your discipline. There are examples of discipline and interdisciplinary examples provided in upcoming chapters to help clarify any important differences in inquiry processes. Ultimately, focusing on the three essential traits of inquiry will provide you with the base you need to get started in inquiry.

How inquiry models can help

Inquiry models:

- represent a holistic view of active knowledge creation.

- attempt to simplify complex learning experiences.

- use "steps" to highlight important distinctions in thinking.

- facilitate thinking important to the discipline.

- focus on the process of knowledge creation rather than the outcome.

- remind learners to pause, stop and think as thinking proceeds and deepens.

- highlight transferable skills.

- stress collaboration at all stages in order to make meaning.

- vary in usefulness according to context.

FIGURE 1.8 Inquiry models can be helpful to learning in many different ways.

THINQ

- What are the similarities and differences between the various inquiry models represented on the next page?

- What other inquiry processes are you familiar with?

- Do you approach a discipline-based inquiry model in your classroom? What benefit, if any, do you see using this approach?

- Which of the processes do you think are most helpful to the learner and why?

Scientific inquiry

| Pose real questions | Find resources | Experiment and explore | Interpret information | Report findings |

FIGURE 1.9 A scientific inquiry model focuses on experimentation and discovery (C. Brunner, 2014).

Mathematical inquiry

Understand the problem

Design a plan

Carry out the plan

Check and extend

FIGURE 1.10 Polya's mathematical inquiry model focuses on solving problems.

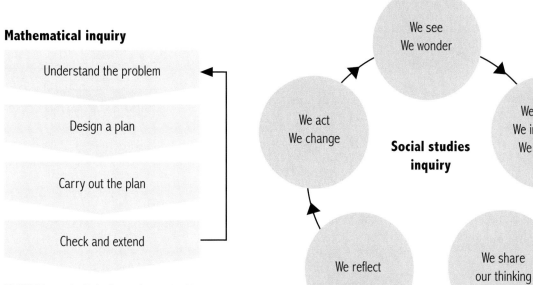

FIGURE 1.11 A social studies inquiry focuses on wondering about, exploring and understanding the world.

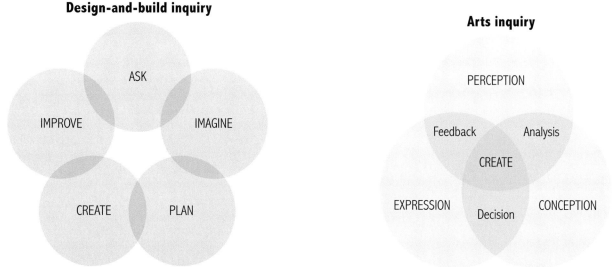

Design-and-build inquiry

ASK

IMAGINE

IMPROVE

CREATE

PLAN

FIGURE 1.12 Design-and-build inquiry models focus on innovation and doing and making things better.

Arts inquiry

PERCEPTION

Feedback

Analysis

CREATE

EXPRESSION

Decision

CONCEPTION

FIGURE 1.13 An arts inquiry or creative process model is focused on the act of creation.

An inquiry model for intermediate learners

An inquiry model for intermediate learners supports and encourages an intellectual journey and character building. Intermediate learners have access to information anywhere, anytime and can connect with people and information in a deep, wide-reaching way. Learning needs to be relevant to their interests and needs, or engagement doesn't really occur. They want to ask questions that interest them. They may be questioning their existing beliefs and considering other perspectives and ways of life. They place great emphasis on what is right and are willing to explore perspectives that challenge their way of thinking.

FIGURE 1.14 Reproducible 1A, p. RE1.

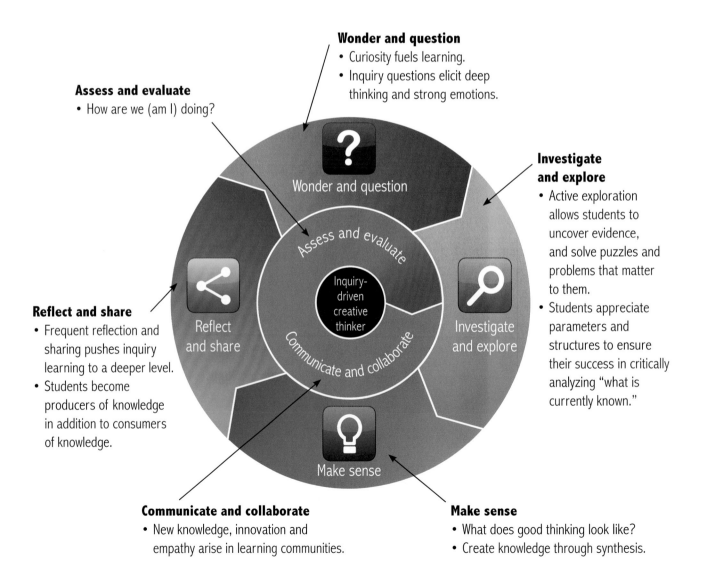

Wonder and question
- Curiosity fuels learning.
- Inquiry questions elicit deep thinking and strong emotions.

Assess and evaluate
- How are we (am I) doing?

Investigate and explore
- Active exploration allows students to uncover evidence, and solve puzzles and problems that matter to them.
- Students appreciate parameters and structures to ensure their success in critically analyzing "what is currently known."

Reflect and share
- Frequent reflection and sharing pushes inquiry learning to a deeper level.
- Students become producers of knowledge in addition to consumers of knowledge.

Communicate and collaborate
- New knowledge, innovation and empathy arise in learning communities.

Make sense
- What does good thinking look like?
- Create knowledge through synthesis.

1.5 What is the intermediate teacher's role in inquiry learning?

BIG IDEA

Inquiry learning is a continuum, with guided inquiry and a large degree of teacher direction at one end, and open inquiry with a large degree of student autonomy at the other end.

An intermediate teacher of inquiry-based learning is someone who brings their excitement for learning to their students. Inquiry-based learning does not require a teacher to know everything, but to be open to learning alongside their students. This teacher can expand upon their personal knowledge base through the work of inquiry and will increase their efficacy in teaching through engagement during the learning process and personal reflection.

They have confidence in their students' abilities and are responsive to their interests. These teachers challenge students to question, think deeper, consider other perspectives and to go beyond the easy answers to find the truth. They seek out conversations with colleagues on the status of inquiries, successes and challenges, as well as brainstorming possible solutions. This teacher is open to feelings of trepidation and is willing to work to overcome these feelings in order to support students in becoming better learners.

CONFIRMATION
In your experience, do children learn best when they are actively involved in "building knowledge"? Why or why not?

Variations in inquiry: From guided to open and everything in between

In speaking with intermediate teachers, we find that misconceptions of inquiry lead to some hesitation in engaging in inquiry-based learning. The most prevalent misconception we come across is that students set off on their own inquiries and the teacher has no control over direction or content. Understandably, this would cause some stress in a teacher who has curriculum to follow and reporting timelines to adhere to. Fortunately, there are variations of inquiry that range in their amount of teacher direction and student autonomy. The most common type falls within the middle of the continuum and is where the teacher and students have a balance of autonomy and independence.

FIGURE 1.15
The inquiry continuum: As you move from guided to open inquiry, the level of student autonomy increases and the level of teacher direction decreases.

Guided, blended and open inquiry refer to the different variations of inquiry that describe the levels of teacher direction and student involvement. At one end of the continuum is guided inquiry. At this end of the continuum there is a high degree of teacher direction and low level of student autonomy. During guided inquiry the teacher may develop the inquiry question and scaffold students throughout the inquiry process.

On the other end of the continuum is open inquiry. In this variation, student autonomy is high and teacher direction is low. There would still be teacher involvement but in more of a consultation role, and as requested by the student. Blended inquiry falls between these two points, with a balance between teacher direction and student involvement, and is often the most common form of inquiry we see in classrooms.

Your knowledge of your students will be the best guide in determining which type of inquiry suits them best. If your students are new to inquiry, they may need to develop an understanding of the inquiry process and require teacher direction on asking questions, investigating and gathering information. This may be where you focus your direct instruction and modelling to ensure students can be successful. On the other hand, some students may need additional support in synthesizing the information to create new knowledge. They may require more support in drawing conclusions and consolidating their thinking, and less in the other stages. It is the teacher, as informed practitioner, who knows where students are, what their needs are and can respond in a timely manner that will determine the level of teacher direction and student autonomy. Ultimately, the goal is to have students develop the skills needed to engage in their own relevant inquiries in their lives, outside of the realm of school.

INQUIRY IN ACTION

Genius Hour

There is a new trend moving through inquiry learning spaces that dedicates time, typically an hour per week, to empowering students to explore their passions. Genius Hour, or Passion Hour, becomes a time for teachers and students to engage in inquiry. This is a great way to start bringing inquiry into the classroom. Students are given one hour a week to pursue their interests or passions and become excited about inquiry. At the same time, this structure provides space for the teacher to engage in inquiry in an intentional way, perhaps as a first step into inquiry-based learning. More information on Genius Hour can be found at www.geniushour.com.

The characteristics of inquiry teaching and teachers

When we talk with teachers who use inquiry learning, we learn a lot from them and about them. Firstly, these teachers believe that they are learning alongside their students and are excited by the prospect of doing so. They are passionate and curious about their disciplines and about critical and creative thought.

They "think big" by identifying essential concepts and skills and they don't abandon these big ideas, even when faced with pressures of coverage, standardized tests and other external mandates. They have confidence in their students' abilities and are responsive to their interests. These teachers take appropriate risks in their teaching by challenging students to think deeper, question, refute, support, interrogate, consider many perspectives, and stretch beyond the obvious and easy-to-answer questions.

These teachers talk about overcoming their own fear and trepidation when conducting an inquiry, caused by the reality that they will never know for sure what may happen. This initial fear changes to excitement over time when they see the benefits to student learning and engagement. These teachers have tried and failed and tried again to create and hone strategies to make their students better inquiry learners.

THINQ

- What supports do you require to implement inquiry-based learning? How will you advocate for these supports?
- Where do you see yourself and your students along the continuum of inquiry?
- How could inquiry be embedded into your professional learning community?

> **COMMITMENT**
> How comfortable are you with the possibility of changing your role as a teacher?

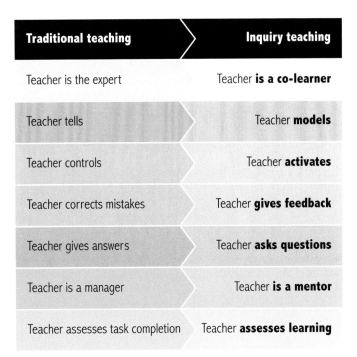

FIGURE 1.16 In an inquiry learning classroom, students benefit when teachers participate as co-learners who model and activate learning.

Inquiry myths and misconceptions

As with any pedagogy, there are myths and misconceptions that invoke barriers for teachers who are interested in exploring inquiry-based learning. Minimizing them means identifying and discussing them together.

COMMITMENT
Do any of these myths and misconceptions limit commitment to inquiry learning in your school?

Inquiry myths and misconceptions	Response
Inquiry is always the best teaching strategy.	A common misconception is that inquiry is the only way to teach. In order for inquiry-based learning to be successful, other strategies need to be in place, including direct instruction, and practicing and mastering literacy and numeracy.
Inquiry takes too much time.	The entire inquiry cycle does not have to be completed in order for learning to happen. Focusing on one aspect of an inquiry method allows you to work with students to develop their skills. Inquiry does take longer than the traditional models; however, big ideas and deeper learning will result.
Inquiry is too unstructured.	Students do not engage in inquiry completely unassisted. Teachers use strategies to develop questioning skills, understanding of the inquiry process and students' responsibility for their learning. When students are actively engaged in their learning and collaborating with peers, it may seem more chaotic.
Inquiry won't engage intermediate students.	Intermediate students can seem passive in their learning. Inquiry offers an alternative learning situation that gives students choice in their inquiries and allows them to take ownership of their learning, ask relevant questions, explore and investigate using technology, and reflect on what they have learned.
Inquiry is difficult to assess.	Inquiry-based learning is most effectively assessed when formative assessment strategies are in place. There do not need to be many new strategies; teachers can apply fundamental assessment for, as and of learning strategies.
Students need more knowledge before they can do an inquiry.	To wait for students to acquire a set skill or memorize certain facts is denying students the opportunity to become active, engaged learners. Teachers get to know their students and recognize the knowledge they come with, and build upon that in collaborative and intentional learning opportunities.

FIGURE 1.17 There are many myths and misconceptions about what inquiry is and how it works.

Exploring ecosystems: Is this inquiry?

As we learned in section 1.4, inquiry learning has three essential traits. Inquiry is grounded in open-ended questions or problems, follows a methodology for thinking and answering the question, and uses creative or critical thinking leading to new knowledge. Let's take a look at Myria's grade 7 science class and consider if she is engaged in an inquiry.

Myria's class is studying the topic of interactions within ecosystems, and she would like to include more inquiry in the unit. They are exploring the complex interactions between organisms and their environment and Myria decides to let students select their own ecosystem to research and construct into a pop-bottle ecosystem. She has provided the students with graphic organizers to support their research. Students will present their findings as well as their pop-bottle ecosystem to the class.

Myria has provided some opportunities for students to have choice in their learning, such as in the type of ecosystem and method of research. In order for it to be a true inquiry, there needs to be a deep inquiry question to guide students on their understanding of the topic. The development of the inquiry question should allow for a more conceptual understanding. For example, "How is our local ecosystem affected by pollution?", "How are ecosystems essential for our survival?" or "Why are ecosystems important?"

To support the development of rich inquiry questions, students would benefit from opportunities to ask deep questions. Myria could have the students brainstorm the questions they have on ecosystems in groups and share them with the class. This would give students an opportunity to select the question(s) that stand out for them, as well as provide the opportunity to critically reflect on the types of questions that spark inquiry.

Requiring students to create pop-bottle ecosystems may not provide them with the opportunity to use their critical thinking skills and synthesize their new knowledge based on the research. Myria could consider giving students more choice in how they share their learning, such as through reports, dioramas, blogs, video reports, or the pop-bottle ecosystem.

To support students through the inquiry process, Myria could consider using a visual model of inquiry to support the process and opportunities for self-reflection (see Reproducible 1A on p. RE1).

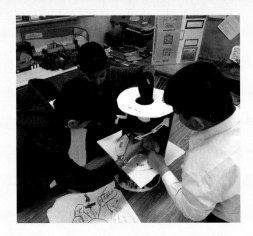

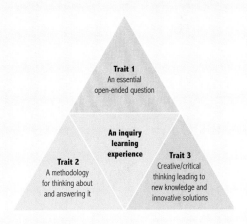

Trait 1
An essential open-ended question

An inquiry learning experience

Trait 2
A methodology for thinking about and answering it

Trait 3
Creative/critical thinking leading to new knowledge and innovative solutions

THINQ

- Which essential traits emerge in Myria's learning experience?

- What modifications could she make to increase student autonomy?

- How could Myria focus the learning to make it a more authentic inquiry experience?

1.6 Are inquiry-based learning and the intermediate learner a good fit?

Inquiry-based learning provides our intermediate learners with the perfect conditions to meet their intellectual and social/emotional learning needs. We can also build upon their inherent strengths and provide support for the unique learning needs of the intermediate learners.

Characteristics and strengths of intermediate learners

Intermediate learners are at an exciting stage of their intellectual journey. They have access to information anywhere, anytime and can connect with people and information in a deep, wide reaching way. Their understanding of the world is open and flat, and this affects the way they seek to learn. This means that learning needs to be relevant to their interests and needs, or engagement doesn't really occur. Of course, this doesn't mean that they are uninterested in learning, just that they want to be a part of it. They want to ask questions that interest them.

Adolescents bring with them a great range of learning strengths, needs, interests, experiences, beliefs, cultures and values. During these years, they experience rapid growth in physical, emotional and cognitive development. McNeely and Blanchard (2009) identify the cognitive, social and emotional implications during this phase of adolescence. Cognitively, students are interested in what is happening in the present and are developing the capacity for abstract thinking. They are beginning to take more risks and their intellectual interests may be expanding. Emotionally, students are developing their own identity and their social relationships begin to have more value. At this stage students are also beginning to test limits and question moral rights and privilege. This truly is an exciting time in their development and inquiry learning enhances the strengths they are developing.

As our students are developing their sense of identity, they are beginning to recognize the importance of identity in their peers. They have an increased desire for social interactions and blossom when this happens in a caring, supportive, responsive and positive classroom climate.

BIG IDEA

Inquiry learning taps into the inherent strengths and intellectual needs of intermediate learners.

FOOD FOR THOUGHT

"Education is a social process; education is growth; education is not preparation for life but is life itself."

John Dewey

CONTEXT

What are the most significant characteristics of your intermediate learners?

They are also faced with getting information quickly, and prefer multi-tasking, engaging in games, role-play and social interactions virtually. This is a stage in which they may be questioning their existing beliefs and considering other perspectives and ways of life. They place great emphasis on what is right and are willing to explore perspectives that challenge their way of thinking.

Connecting to the lives and experiences of intermediate students

When learning connects to the lives and experiences of students, it provides an opening for engagement. When students' cultures, identities, lives and experiences are invited into the classroom, they become more engaged in their learning, more understanding of their peers and others' experiences, and will pursue learning connected to their relevant interests. Here are just a few examples of inquiries intermediate students have engaged in that reflect their identity, lives and experiences:

- How does my identity impact my feelings of belonging at home and at school?

- What problem in my school or community do I want to solve?

- What innovation would impact the life of someone important to me?

- How does gender stereotyping in the media affect my self-esteem?

- Why do inequalities still exist in my community?

- How could our school (or the education system, or the curriculum) be improved?

- Should I quit social media to improve my mental well-being?

THINQ

- How could utilizing students' interests impact the inquiry experience?

- In what ways could you make the inquiry process relevant to your students?

INQUIRY IN ACTION

Solving real problems

Inquiry learning can take place throughout the school, inside and outside of the classroom. Todd, a grade 8 teacher, and his students turned inquiry into action. They explored ways to address student safety during the high volume of street traffic before and after school. One group of students identified alternative transportation as an option to reduce traffic. During their research, they learned that many students did not ride their bikes to school because the bikes were in need of repair. With the support of another teacher, they began a bike repair club. The club now offers repair service to students throughout the school, increasing the number of students who ride their bikes to school.

Helping intermediate students understand inquiry

While our intermediate students come to us with many strengths, we may also need to work with them to understand inquiry learning and their role in the process. Inquiry learning often requires students to be more active, and if they understand why inquiry learning is important they will be more apt to embrace the change.

Developing a strong understanding of inquiry will open the doors for more active participation. Engaging students through a provocation or inquiry exploration task will provide them with the basis for recognizing what interests them, the types of deep questions they can ask, as well as possibilities for ways to answer these deep questions.

To spark curiosity in your students, find out what they are interested in. Sharing your own curiosity is a great way to get the conversation started. Moving on to what makes students curious will help spark students into seeing themselves as inquiry learners. Prompts to promote discussion on curiosity could be used as an exit ticket post-discussion or used as a group brainstorming session on inquiry learner traits.

Reproducibles 1B, 1C, 1D and 1E provide prompts to help engage students in understanding inquiry, curiosity and seeing themselves as inquiry learners. These reproducibles could also be used in a variety of ways, such as a prompt in a community circle, sentence starters in a think-pair-share, in an interview scenario or exit ticket.

> **CONTEXT**
> How well do you think your students understand inquiry?

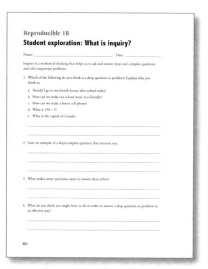

FIGURES 1.18–1.21
Reproducibles 1B, 1C, 1D and 1E, pp. RE2–RE5.

"Who am I?" Exploring identity through teacher and student inquiry

Teacher inquiry can have a powerful impact on pedagogical practice, teaching, learning and school climate. In this example, a student inquiry stemmed from a teacher inquiry focused on student voice.

Raley and two of her colleagues were invited to attend a professional learning series with their school board. The focus of the sessions was on incorporating student voice into the classroom through creating art. Working with the Arts and Equity instructional leaders, they developed an inquiry plan and began their research to understand student voice, identity and belonging, and the impact these qualities had on classroom and school climate.

Raley, who taught visual and dramatic arts, decided to introduce the concept of identity to her students. To explore and gain insight into their own identity and how others perceived their identity, they engaged in role-playing and self-reflection activities. These included brainstorming the many roles they play (e.g., "I am a daughter," "I am the youngest child," etc.), creating life maps, and using role play to explore alternative perspectives. Read-aloud texts and TED Talks provided alternative ways to explore why identity is important. As students moved into their artistic inquiry, they were given the concept of identity and the inquiry question "Who am I?" Using a planning template, students developed their artistic plan to create a piece (visual or dramatic) that represented a component of their identity. Students had choice in medium and format for their work and this resulted in a wide range of portraits, sculptures and video narratives. When the artistic piece was completed, students shared their artistic statements, reflecting on their inquiry question to synthesize and consolidate their learning.

To connect the student inquiry back to the teacher inquiry, students shared their art and statements with the school community. This continued the conversation on identity and why sharing their identity stories is important to classroom and school culture.

THINQ

- How does this inquiry honour student voice?
- Consider a learning activity you do with your students that involves inquiry. How could you modify the activity to deepen the connection to students' culture, identity, lives and experiences?
- How could you and your colleagues engage in collaborative inquiry to develop more of a reflective stance within your school?

Revisit and reflect

This introductory chapter explored what inquiry learning is and how it benefits the intermediate learner. This is a dynamic process that remains relevant today and develops skills that have real-world applications for students today and for the future. We discussed how inquiry learning benefits the learner by actively engaging them in the process of learning and allows the teacher to learn alongside the students and become a skillful facilitator in the inquiry journey. In the next chapter we will look at the assessment of inquiry and how teachers can best support students as they learn through inquiry.

THINQ

- What interests you most about inquiry-based learning?

- Do you think inquiry-based learning is appropriate during the information age? Why or why not?

- Describe your greatest barrier to implementing inquiry-based learning. What ideas from this chapter could help you overcome these challenges?

- What types of inquiry are at the forefront of your school and your school district?

- Consider Reproducible 1F, *Teacher self-assessment: Inquiry readiness checklist.* How ready are you?

BIG IDEAS

1.1 We learn by asking questions (inquiring) and are constantly creating new knowledge because knowledge is personally and socially constructed.

1.2 Central to inquiry learning are beliefs about who learners are and what they are capable of.

1.3 Inquiry dispositions support risk-taking and a sustainable commitment to inquiry learning.

1.4 Inquiry learning, regardless of grade or discipline, has three common essential traits.

1.5 Inquiry learning is a continuum, with guided inquiry and a large degree of teacher direction at one end, and open inquiry with a large degree of student autonomy at the other end.

1.6 Inquiry learning taps into the inherent strengths and intellectual needs of intermediate learners.

Reproducible 1F

Teacher self-assessment: Inquiry readiness checklist

Check which of the following statements represents your knowledge, beliefs and understanding of inquiry learning. Use this checklist for self-reflection, for planning and sharing with colleagues, and to determine next steps in deepening your inquiry practice.

Conviction
- I believe in the main assumptions of inquiry-based learning: that learning is constructivist, student-centred and demands critical thinking.
- I am familiar with and convinced by the research that supports inquiry to improve student engagement and learning.

Commitment
- I am committed to bringing more inquiry-based learning to my classroom and have reflected on not only what makes me excited about inquiry learning, but also what makes me uncertain.
- I have connected with other committed educators who are interested and supportive of inquiry education.

Capacity
- I understand that inquiry is a process used to answer questions, solve problems and make new knowledge.
- I understand that a guided inquiry is a highly-structured and thoughtfully designed endeavour that allows for optimal student autonomy.
- I know there are distinct stages involved in an inquiry process.
- I understand that there are many inquiry models to choose from but that these models share essential traits.
- I understand that inquiries are on a continuum from guided to open (and that a degree of guidance is essential for effective student learning).

Context
- I understand what my role should be in an inquiry classroom.
- I accept that inquiry learning in my classroom should be "playful," "messy," complex, recursive, iterative, non-linear experience and not merely a lock-step process to completing a product.
- I have thought about my students' readiness for inquiry and know where to start.

Confirmation
- I know what my professional goals are with respect to doing more inquiry.
- I understand how I will assess my progress, what is working and how to improve.

RE6

FIGURE 1.22 Reproducible 1F, p. RE6.

Chapter 2

ASSESSMENT AND EVALUATION:
Understanding how our intermediate learners are doing

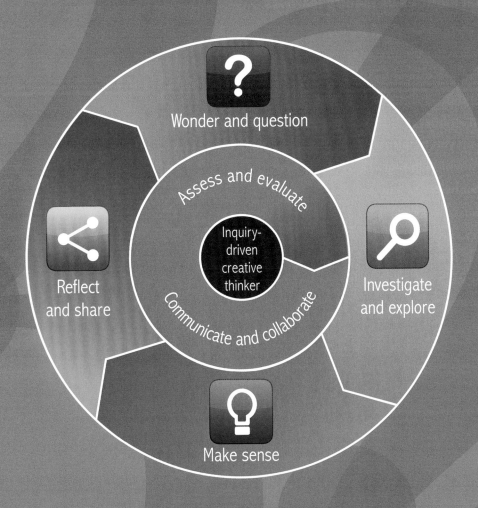

2.1 What is inquiry assessment?

Assessment should be a frequent and meaningful time for the student and teacher to pause and reflect on where they are in their learning journey.

The question "Where am I?" allows the individual to reflect on his or her inquiry progress as well as identify what the next steps are. Collectively, the teacher and student can ask "Where are we?" in order to re-focus the inquiry of the classroom community. When we take this time to pause and ask these questions, whether individually or collectively, we are in a place where we can empower and improve learning.

These core questions can be revised to be more specific to the inquiry or focus. However, even in their most general form, they allow the student and teacher to reflect frequently on where they are and what they need to do to get where they are going.

BIG IDEA

At the heart of assessment are teachers and students asking, "How are we doing?"

CONVICTION
How important is it to you that your students develop these skills?

Six essential abilities of inquiry learners

We consider these six essential abilities to be the core of inquiry activities and inquiry assessment. While each inquiry should be unique, we find it is helpful to have these essential abilities in mind in order to help you frame your inquiry assessment planning. These six abilities can help you and your students understand what is at the core of inquiry. These essential abilities can lay the foundation for your planning of whole-class guided inquiry or for more independent inquiry learning experiences for students.

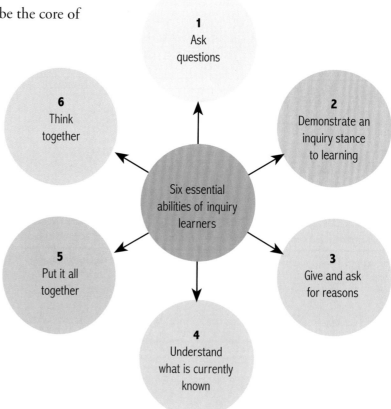

1 Ask questions
2 Demonstrate an inquiry stance to learning
3 Give and ask for reasons
4 Understand what is currently known
5 Put it all together
6 Think together

Six essential abilities of inquiry learners

FIGURE 2.1 Assessing inquiry means assessing and improving the essential abilities of students as inquiry learners.

Asks questions

The first essential ability of inquiry learners focuses on a student's ability to ask questions. This is a vital skill and the basis for all other essential abilities. For example, when we put it all together, we are asking students to synthesize the information they have gathered, ask questions to clarify meaning and stretch their thinking. This process of asking questions will also allow learners and teachers to collectively uncover their beliefs and offer an alternative perspective, innovate or create something new. When we understand what is currently known, we use our questioning skills to determine credibility, point of view and authority of the information. Chapter 3, *Wondering and questioning*, provides more information on questioning and assessing this essential inquiry skill.

Demonstrates an inquiry stance

Demonstrating an inquiry stance to learning is an essential ability that connects to the learning dispositions we explored in Chapter 1, *Getting started*. When we demonstrate an inquiry learning stance, we are demonstrating curiosity, criticality, hopefulness and open-mindedness. While we have highlighted four inquiry learning dispositions, it is up to you to decide which you will choose to focus on. Inquiry dispositions should have meaning to your students, and be selected based upon your specific focus within the classroom or in connection to your school, board, district or ministry priorities.

To support your discussions on inquiry dispositions, we have included Reproducible 2A, *How to model and assess inquiry dispositions* for you to use with your students.

FOOD FOR THOUGHT

"One student may see feedback as sending the message 'you're not smart enough,' while another student may see the same feedback as saying 'you're not smart enough — yet'. What matters is whether students see their future potential as limited by their current performance or not. Students who believe that ability is fixed will see any piece of work as a chance either to reaffirm their ability or to be shown up. If they are confident in their ability to achieve what is asked of them, then they will attempt the task. However, if their confidence in their ability to carry out their task is low, they may well avoid the challenge (especially if they think others will succeed) and this can be seen in classrooms every day."

Dylan Wiliam

"Although the universal teacher lament that there's no time for such feedback is understandable, remember that 'no time to give and use feedback' actually means 'no time to cause learning.' As we have seen, research shows that less teaching plus more feedback is the key to achieving greater learning. And there are numerous ways — through technology, peers, and other teachers — that students can get the feedback they need. So try it out. Less teaching, more feedback."

Grant Wiggins

"The new pedagogies require a teacher to have a repertoire of strategies, which may range from project-based learning through direct instruction to an inquiry-based model. But the key is that the teacher takes a highly proactive role in driving the learning process forward, using whichever strategy works for a specific student or task (and analyzing which strategy works best). In the new pedagogies this means interacting with students to make the students' thinking and questions about learning more visible."

John Hattie

This reproducible defines the dispositions and offers suggestions on what they may look like in your classroom. It also outlines how inquiry-based learning supports these dispositions and includes prompts for student reflection that can be used as a student self-assessment.

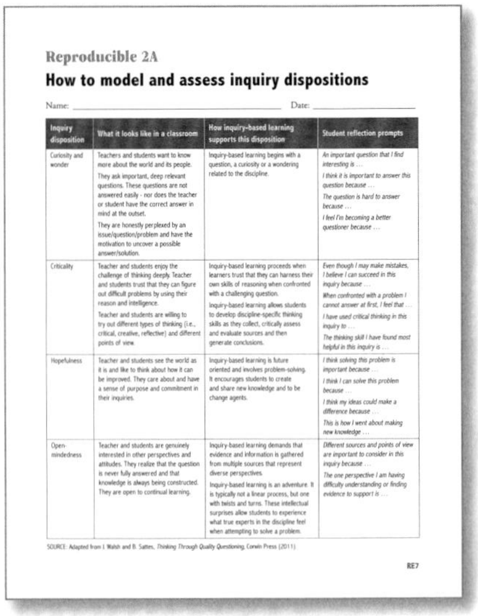

FIGURE 2.2 Reproducible 2A, p. RE7.

Gives reasons

When we ask students to give and ask for reasons, we are asking them to engage in high-level critical thinking processes, which can include conceptualizing, analyzing, synthesizing and evaluating. These higher level critical thinking skills can be focused on in greater detail within a particular unit or throughout the inquiry process.

Understands what is currently known

The fourth essential ability, understand what is currently known, narrows in on students' understanding of content knowledge. Chapter 4, *Investigating and exploring*, provides more detail on assessing this essential ability and is where we explore the ways students gather and use information at this stage of the inquiry process.

> **CONTEXT**
> What are the current skills and abilities of your students as inquiry learners?

Puts it together

Applying what is known and drawing and communicating conclusions is highlighted in our fifth essential ability, putting it all together. At this stage, students work towards synthesizing all of the information they have collected and will begin looking for patterns or trends. Chapter 5, *Making sense*, takes a deeper look at assessing the essential ability of putting it all together.

Thinks together

The final essential inquiry ability is how we think together. This ability connects to the "reflect and share" stage of the inquiry process and is an opportunity for students to share their new knowledge and push the thinking even deeper by reflecting on their conclusions. It asks students to think together to build on each other's new ideas, to assist in drawing inferences and to identify their own assumptions and beliefs. The opportunity to think for themselves and to think cooperatively allows students to see beyond their own conclusions and perspectives and elicit additional reflection, shifting the inquiry even deeper. Chapter 6, *Reflection and sharing*, provides more detail on the essential ability of thinking together.

These essential abilities offer you the base of your inquiry assessment plan. If you feel they are a good place to start your inquiry planning, determine what excellence would look like in each ability and plan some learning activities that could allow you to gather evidence on these abilities. Reproducible 2B, *The six essential inquiry abilities for assessment* may support you in your initial planning.

Inquiry dispositions

It is worth mentioning that while inquiry dispositions are not included in most curricula, these are essential skills that will support students as they engage in inquiry and in their journey as a life-long learner. These skills often get overlooked in assessments and are typically not given the investment they deserve in classrooms. We believe that inquiry learning involves not just the academic but the social, and that inquiry dispositions are a form of social learning. Inquiry-based learning moves beyond isolated skills or information. It is our belief that inquiry dispositions influence a student's ability to become strong, creative, knowledge-seeking thinkers. They will help a child develop their individual identity as learners and their future potential in our rapidly changing, knowledge-rich world.

Having the opportunity to discuss real-life examples of inquiry learners from their communities will enhance students' understanding of who is an inquiry learner. Reproducible 2C, *Student exploration: Who is an inquiry learner?* may be a starting point for students to begin defining the abilities of inquiry learners.

THINQ

- How could the six essential abilities of an inquiry learner help teachers and students understand what is at the crux of inquiry learning?

- How could your students self-assess their own learning goals in relation to the six essential abilities?

- How do the six essential abilities of an inquiry learner connect to your mandated curriculum?

- How could you use the six essential abilities of an inquiry learner to support the planning of formative and summative assessments?

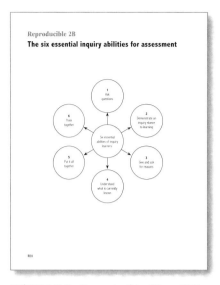

FIGURE 2.3 Reproducible 2B, p. RE8.

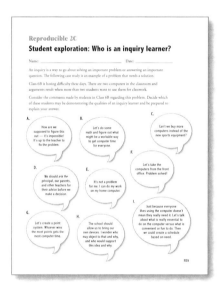

FIGURE 2.4 Reproducible 2C, p. RE9.

2.2 How do I assess what is essential to inquiry along with everything else?

We regularly hear from teachers that they struggle to teach and assess all of the content and skills prescribed in the curriculum. As controversial as this may sound, we feel that it is virtually impossible to "cover" the curriculum through learning and assessment activities in any deep, meaningful way. It is challenging trying to figure out how to teach and assess "all" the information and skills of any history, science, health or music topic. Often we default to what we are interested in or skilled at as teachers, resort to previous practice, or make decisions to cover what is supported by available resources. So how do we assess the curriculum as well as inquiry abilities and skills? We would like to share two starting points for assessment that are based in our work with teams of teachers across subject and grade levels.

Inquiry and the curriculum

We suggest that you first locate essential inquiry skills and dispositions within the assessment and evaluation tools mandated by your school, district or region. These may include performance standards for assessment such as knowledge, thinking, communication and application. Reproducible 2D, *An inquiry rubric: What are the specific characteristics of a successful inquiry?* provides a sample framework of how inquiry can be assessed and evaluated according to the field of knowledge and skills as an example.

Secondly, we suggest that once you map your inquiry skills and dispositions onto mandated assessment and evaluation, you dive into the curriculum to identify inquiry learning and begin your planning. While each region is different, this second step will help you find that some curricula (e.g., math, science, geography and language arts) are explicit at identifying the inquiry skills and processes to be developed. In others, inquiry may not be explicitly identified but can be found in critical thinking expectations, problem-solving processes, collaboration, innovation and other creative processes.

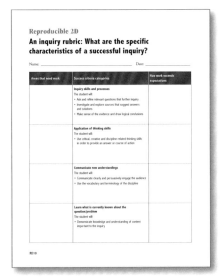

FIGURE 2.5 Reproducible 2D, p. RE10.

Mapping out explicit and implicit inquiry skills across subject areas can be a valuable conversation between teachers in the intermediate division. If you are teaching a subject-specific discipline, having conversations with colleagues both inside and outside of the discipline can create a clear focus for developing inquiry skills in students. Use the six essential abilities as a framework to group and assess the required curriculum or standards. If, as a team, you decide to focus on questioning as the first essential inquiry ability you want to foster, you could co-create criteria related to questioning and design an assessment tool to target those criteria. This approach could offer your students and colleagues a clear focus on assessing inquiry. See Reproducible 2E, *Assessment planning template: Asks questions* as an example.

Many teachers find that a single topic or unit is a good place to introduce or expand inquiry thinking for their students. This could be within a unit of science, history, geography or health and well-being. Literacy and numeracy skills are easily incorporated into inquiry learning. If you are more experienced, you may want to deepen and extend inquiry learning by increasing student choice and independence. You may wish to set aside a certain amount of time per week to encourage students to pursue their own inquiries independently. This type of inquiry, called "genius hour" or "personal passion projects," are described in greater detail in Chapter 1, *Getting started*.

It is our belief that curriculum should be seen as a means, not as an end. If our goal is to engage students in deep, rich and personally relevant learning activities, then we need to see the curriculum as a way to carry the learning forward. Inquiry learning reminds us that what is known on a certain topic is only provisional. Knowledge is constantly changing because inquiry learners are constantly building upon this knowledge.

THINQ

- How could you and your colleagues begin to plan meaningful inquiry assessment based on the six essential abilities?

- Where are the explicit and implicit inquiry skills and dispositions in your curriculum, and in recent evidence-based education trends?

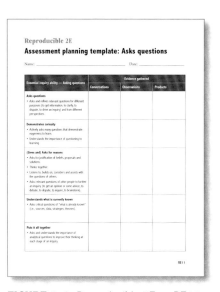

FIGURE 2.6 Reproducible 2E, p. RE11.

2.3 How can we engage intermediate learners in assessment?

Intermediate students should be our assessment partners. Effective assessment partnerships are meaningful to both teachers and students, motivate students to higher levels of achievement and help students develop the capacity for self-assessment.

Students should understand what is being assessed, what to aim for, what quality looks like, and be provided choice in how they demonstrate their learning. When we invite students to be partners with us throughout the assessment and learning process, they will experience a connectedness to the learning, become more engaged with the inquiry and be more willing to share their learning with their peers.

Engaging learners

Involving students in building success criteria will help develop a deeper understanding of what they need to do to demonstrate the required skill or concept. Using the six essential inquiry abilities is a place to begin your assessment partnership with intermediate students.

With your students you can determine what "quality" looks like in each of the inquiry abilities. Consulting with students on their growth in these abilities will help strengthen their autonomy in developing these skills. Students can be a part of the discussion on how they will demonstrate these skills and what type of evidence they might want to show to demonstrate they are meeting the criteria for these inquiry skills. Consider how peers could be involved in this assessment process for developing these skills.

The use of journals or portfolios (digital, audio and/or written) that provide evidence of the six abilities may help you in developing your inquiry assessment partnerships. There are many technologies that you and students may choose that allow students to capture and share their thinking with peers, teachers and parents.

BIG IDEA

Students should be our assessment partners.

CONTEXT
To what degree are your students engaged in their own assessment?

WORDS MATTER

We have included a list of essential inquiry vocabulary in Reproducible 2F, *Essential inquiry vocabulary*. It offers a list of words that can be used to support a shared understanding of inquiry learning and the development of inquiry success criteria.

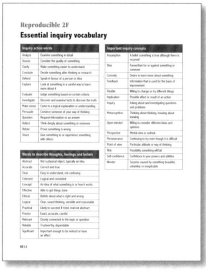

FIGURE 2.7 Reproducible 2F, p. RE12.

Our ultimate goal in inquiry assessment is for students to internalize the six essential inquiry abilities so they can assess their own work and understand what they need to do to improve. For example, when we ask our intermediate learners to think together, we ask questions to clarify meaning, stretch thinking, uncover beliefs and offer alternative perspectives. While our intermediate learners may have an understanding of what it means to critically evaluate the information they have collected, they may still be developing their analytical skills. For example, developing criteria with students on making connections between personal ideas and evidence will give them a clearer understanding of putting it all together.

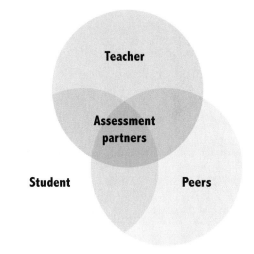

CONVICTION
Do you believe that effective inquiry assessment is best achieved when the teacher, students and their peers work together to improve learning?

Building assessment partnerships

Throughout all stages of the inquiry process, students will benefit from effective feedback. Feedback should be a dynamic process where the student understands where they are in their learning, where they need to go and what they need to do to get there. As mentioned in Chapter 1, *Getting started*, classroom communities that are rich in feedback will help students develop richer inquiry questions, go deeper with their investigation and synthesis, and effectively share their new knowledge with their classmates and peers.

Effective assessment involves the teacher, the student and peers. When the teacher and peers become partners within the assessment process, students can provide valuable feedback on the inquiry, for example, when:

- Student self-assessment focuses on the individual's ability to understand their learning goal and success criteria, and use these to judge what they have learned and what they still need to learn.

- Peer-to-peer feedback involves students giving feedback to each other on their work as it connects to the success criteria. This would focus on what has been done well, what still needs to be done, as well as advice on how to improve.

- Teacher feedback is grounded in the success criteria and tells the student where they are in their learning, what they have achieved, where they need to go and how they might get there.

FIGURE 2.8 Effective inquiry assessment is best achieved when teachers, students and their peers work together to improve learning. These three partnerships in the assessment process should take place on an ongoing basis through all stages of the inquiry.

A feedback-rich classroom

Providing effective feedback is a crucial component of formative assessment. Research on the importance of formative assessment details how effective feedback can increase student achievement. When feedback is accepted and acted upon by the learner, it leads to higher achievement. Effective feedback is not praise or highlighting misconceptions or deficiencies. It needs to be specific to the inquiry learning skills and dispositions, be helpful to individual learners and provide them with a course of action to take.

Giving effective feedback is a skill, and all learners can be vulnerable when receiving it. This highlights the importance of establishing a culture of respect and trust as outlined in Chapter 1, *Getting started*. Establishing norms of collaboration and feedback will help set the tone for a learner to give and receive feedback. Feedback should make the learner think, and be given in a respectful and timely manner. The case study: *Co-creating success criteria for an inquiry* highlights one way to develop a classroom into a feedback-rich classroom. Developing a common understanding of inquiry dispositions and the criteria for inquiry will give students the language they need to effectively and respectfully respond to each other throughout the inquiry process.

Strategies for giving effective feedback

1. Use technology (e.g., audio, video, photos and document sharing) to facilitate "real time" self and peer feedback.

2. When posting the criteria of quality work for a particular inquiry, be sure to return to the list throughout the inquiry process to allow students to revise the list based on new learning in the class.

3. Provide students with exemplars of work and ask them to provide written or oral feedback based on one or two criteria. Take samples of the feedback and use it for a class discussion on the qualities of effective feedback.

4. Highlight (do not annotate) a student's written work and return it to them, asking them to determine what criteria of quality was highlighted and how it could be improved.

5. Ask students to create a written paragraph or oral presentation to highlight their argument and supporting evidence, or any other relevant criteria for quality.

6. When students submit work to you, ask them to identify one criteria that they would like for you to provide feedback on (this feedback could differ from criteria used in self or peer assessment).

7. Provide students with checklists of basic requirements that they must complete before work is assessed. Return work that does not meet the checklist requirements (do not assess it). Checklist requirements may include: the work is word-processed; the work has been proofread; the work includes a title, a main argument and three sources (at least one from a library book), etc.

8. Postpone, for as long as possible, putting levels, marks or grades on assessment pieces. Descriptive feedback is what is most helpful for the learner at this stage.

9. If a student is not responding to feedback, ask them if they need something to be re-taught or re-explained and/or provide other emotional-social supports.

10. Encourage students to explain criteria and to ask for feedback from parents, guardians and caregivers.

11. Before you provide extensive written feedback to students, ask yourself whether the learner has had opportunities to self-assess based on criteria for quality that they understand.

FIGURE 2.9 There are many ways to provide effective feedback to your students.

Co-creating success criteria for an inquiry

Ronin wants to co-construct the success criteria for an inquiry with his students so they understand what is expected of them during the process and for the final product. He has taken time to reflect on his own inquiry readiness and has explored the prior knowledge his students bring to the inquiry process and identified their inquiry dispositions. Through his initial assessment of students' readiness, Ronin has identified that a few students have experience with inquiry; however, most are new to it. He realizes that in order to create success criteria for inquiry, he must have an idea of what success in inquiry looks like himself. Being prepared in this way will not only allow him to develop his own understanding of what success looks like, but he now has some criteria in his back pocket to help guide students.

The criteria Ronin has in mind are framed in student-friendly language:

- I have developed a rich question to guide my inquiry.
- I understand the knowledge and information important to the inquiry.
- I have gathered and analyzed information from a variety of sources and perspectives.
- I understand that other perspectives may be missing from my sources and I will search for more information when needed.
- I understand my sources, including the main idea, arguments and their position, and I can explain these clearly.
- I have developed, selected and used relevant criteria in order to successfully answer my inquiry question.
- I have enough information gathered to answer my inquiry question.

Ronin introduces a visual model of an inquiry process and invites students to think about what each stage may look like based on a real-life example of an inquiry that involves making a decision: "You are thinking about buying a new cell phone. How will you decide which is best? What questions will you ask and to whom? What information will you gather? How will you make a decision?"

Students share their answers and Ronin highlights how their responses fit into the inquiry process visual he shared with them. For example, Ronin responds to a student who says, "I'd ask my uncle for his opinion because he's a techie and always has the latest gadgets," by showing her how this is called "analyzing a source." To another student who asks "What features do you need on the phone?" he explains that this is using judgment.

Ronin has his students elaborate on what is a successful versus an unsuccessful inquiry. He then poses a deeper question that students are familiar with and repeats the process of considering the stages of a successful inquiry. Finally he returns to the inquiry process graphic and has students generate one or two specific criteria for a successful inquiry under the following four headings:

- Posing a question
- Understanding what is already known
- Gathering evidence
- Proposing a solution and communicating new understandings

He helps students refine the criteria as needed by asking, extending and clarifying questions. His students see that an inquiry is rooted in open questions and demands they think deeply, research effectively and respond clearly. He posts a preliminary version of inquiry success criteria and will continue to refine it as they work through the inquiry process as needed.

Direct instruction and modelling of effective feedback is sometimes overlooked. Students need to understand how to give effective feedback. When a teacher models this process and deconstructs it, students will be more prepared to give effective feedback and less praise (e.g., "I like your illustrations") or criticism (e.g., "Your point doesn't make any sense"). These latter types of feedback do not provide the receiver with possible improvements.

CONTEXT
Do you sometimes feel that you spend more time giving feedback than students spend addressing it?

Students also need to learn how to receive and question feedback (e.g., "What do you mean when you say you like my poster?") and possibly how to reject unreasonable feedback (e.g., "I gave you three strong arguments. Why don't you think they are all strong?"). This ability connects nicely with inquiry reasoning skills.

A classroom rich in effective feedback connects the learner, the teacher and the peer in a relationship of reciprocity. As a student, if I am given opportunities to give feedback to other learners, it allows me to share in the learning, and to reflect on my own learning. Getting feedback from my peers allows me to have another set of eyes on my work. When I engage in a conversation with my teacher and peers, we can develop our understanding of criteria for quality. I will also expect my fellow learners to put forth their best effort when giving feedback and I will respond by improving my work because I value their feedback.

Another aspect of achieving a classroom rich in effective feedback is ensuring that students have time to receive and give feedback, and then have the opportunity to implement the feedback.

Finding time can be challenging; however, the quality of work will be affected greatly when students have time to review, reflect and implement feedback. It is well worth the effort. Figure 2.9 provides a list of suggestions on how to use feedback effectively during inquiry learning.

Determining what students already know

Knowing where your students are in their inquiry learning is vital for planning and supporting your students. Determining if your students have prior inquiry learning experience and any rudimentary inquiry learning skills will help support the implementation of inquiry-based learning within the classroom. It is only too easy to dive into inquiry activities without knowing if your students understand the difference between a deep question versus a shallow one, a summary versus a synthesis, and a question versus a hypothesis.

We have included a number of reproducibles to help you gather information on what your students already know about inquiry. Reproducible 2G, *Student exploration: Can you identify an argument?* and Reproducible 2H, *Student explorations: Errors in thinking and logic* are two activities you can do with students to help you gather information on inquiry abilities before they are asked to apply it in a more sophisticated way. For example, your students may come to class thinking that an argument is when two people yell at each other. This misconception is a natural starting place to unpack and develop the concept of an argument as an essential part of reasoning and to help students make their own arguments and consider the arguments of others.

Reproducible 2H, *Student exploration: Errors in thinking and logic* is a starting place to find out what your students think is strong or weak thinking. You may be surprised by how easily students are able to identify strong thinking. The challenge for students and adults alike is to become self-reflective and recognize when we are not thinking strongly. It's easier to identify weaknesses in others' arguments; however, to strengthen our own, we need to think deeply.

As you have students work through the two reproducibles, your observations and the resulting conversations will assist you in determining the next steps, which could include direct instruction, additional examples or additional practice. You will know if students are ready to move on to develop their own arguments or are capable of recognizing arguments from more complicated sources, like the Internet. Providing students with an opportunity to summarize their key findings or create a key visual in an inquiry journal may provide you with additional assessment data.

THINQ

- How do you create classroom conditions where students are confident and comfortable in giving, receiving and questioning feedback?

- In what ways are your students partners in the assessment process? What will you do to develop this partnership?

- What methods of feedback do you feel most comfortable with? Which new methods would you like to try?

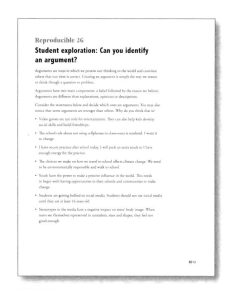

FIGURE 2.10 Reproducible 2G, p. RE13.

FIGURE 2.11 Reproducible 2H, p. RE14.

2.4 How do I gather, interpret and respond to assessment evidence?

Inquiry assessment is a three stage, iterative process that involves gathering, interpreting and responding to evidence of the quality of a student's inquiry skills and dispositions. When we gather enough evidence of each student achieving their best, we can be confident in our assessment of the inquiry.

So how do we plan to gather enough evidence to assess and support all learners? How do we ensure that each student is represented in ways that are fair and reflective? One of the most basic ways is to triangulate your data. This means that the data you collect is balanced between observations of the student, conversations with the student and the products of learning created by the student.

Balanced assessment

Traditionally, assessment has been based primarily on tests and projects. Teachers have an extensive list of products that could be used as assessment evidence, such as oral presentations, web pages, blogs, dioramas, models, performances and artwork. However, these are only valid forms of assessment when they genuinely reflect the student's best thinking and full understanding.

You may recall a student who was not particularly adept at or motivated to create a certain product. However, when you engaged in conversation with them or observed them working collaboratively with others, you noticed that they knew much more and had considerably more skill than their product captured. When we capture multiple examples of observations, conversations and products, we are able to paint a clearer, more equitable picture of the learner. Teachers are also able to react more quickly to conversations and observations, and provide timely and practical feedback.

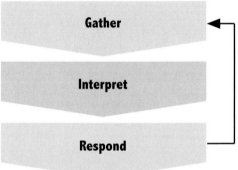

FIGURE 2.12 There are three stages to the inquiry assessment process.

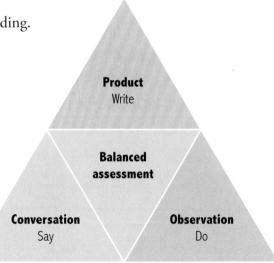

FIGURE 2.13 Balanced assessment means gathering evidence of learning through observation and conversation, not just written products.

Observations and conversations are not only powerful formative assessment tools but also can be used as evaluative assessment. For example, if a student is able to demonstrate logical thinking during a small group discussion, or articulate their logic in a one-on-one conversation, then this evidence is valid. If they are unable to demonstrate their logic for a similar problem during a written task, they may require support with word choice, organizing their thinking or confidence in their ability to write.

As we move into the second stage of the iterative inquiry assessment process, we begin interpreting the evidence we have gathered. In order to increase the validity of our interpretation, we must make sure that the criteria of quality are understood by the learner in advance. Co-creating the criteria and providing timely feedback based on the criteria will ensure that our assessment is more valid.

During the third stage of the inquiry assessment process, we respond to the evidence of learning we have gathered and interpreted. Consider the question: Can you carry on with the next task confident in the student's abilities, or do you need to provide additional feedback or perhaps redesign your teaching next steps?

Throughout these three stages of inquiry assessment, our decisions will have an impact on our goal of gathering evidence of students achieving their best work at a given point in time, positively or negatively. This is an exciting, creative aspect of teaching — deciding what pedagogical moves you will make to provide the best instructional and assessment methods for your students. The beauty of inquiry learning is that you have the time and opportunity to observe students learning, engage the learner in conversations and provide feedback that moves their learning forward as you proceed through an inquiry.

> **CONVICTION**
> How convinced are you that a balanced approach to gathering evidence of learning is fairer and more reliable than one based largely on written work? What else do you need to know?

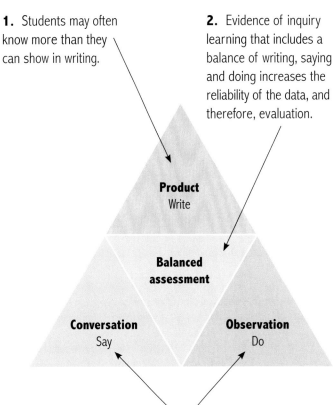

1. Students may often know more than they can show in writing.

2. Evidence of inquiry learning that includes a balance of writing, saying and doing increases the reliability of the data, and therefore, evaluation.

3. Some inquiry learning goals can only be effectively assessed by watching and listening.

FIGURE 2.14 There are three very important reasons why a balanced approach to inquiry assessment is essential to gathering valid and reliable evidence of student learning.

Capturing evidence of student learning through pedagogical documentation

In the previous section we considered what balanced assessment looks like and how we can use the three-stage inquiry assessment process to gather, interpret and respond to the quality of inquiry skills and dispositions. We explored the use of observations, conversations and products to provide a balanced triangulated assessment of inquiry. Pedagogical documentation is a process that enhances assessment of inquiry learning, student voice and the educator's response. So what makes documentation pedagogical? According to some, "… [P]art of what makes documentation pedagogical is the careful, iterative process of examining and responding to the interplay between learning, the educator's pedagogical decisions, and the student's role and voice in the learning" ("Pedagogical Documentation Revisited," 2015).

Pedagogical documentation drives a deeper analysis of the student learning experience through the three phases of inquiry assessment. The process of pedagogical documentation can be framed into three stages and aligns nicely with our inquiry assessment process: (1) *gather:* observing and capturing the student learning experience; (2) *interpret:* collaborative interpretation; and (3) *respond:* responding and sharing.

TECH-ENABLED INQUIRY

Apps to support documentation

There are many different apps you can use to capture, store and share your documentation. During our work, teachers from the early years through high school have shared a multitude of apps that can be used. Consider your audience for the documentation — are you using the platforms to engage parents in the inquiry and assessment process, are you looking to promote dialogue between students, or are you using these tools for your own professional development or inquiry? Here we highlight a few of the most popular. Each offers slightly different features and purpose; ultimately you will need to find what works best for you.

G Suite For Education offers many features that support documentation. Many school boards are connected with G Suite and offer large digital storage. Google Drive allows you to create a folder system to organize your data. Google Docs give you a platform to work collaboratively online and Google Classroom offers a virtual classroom where students can collaborate. https://edu.google.com/trust/

Seesaw provides a way to display student work online, as well as link the images to each student so you can maintain a chronological record of your documentation. This platform also allows you to share images with parents and have them comment on the images their child is tagged in. https://web.seesaw.me

Evernote allows you to save notes and insert images into the notes. These can be saved in an online portfolio format that can be shared with students or parents. https://evernote.com

Fresh Grade facilitates the sharing of student work with parents, allowing them to follow their child's progress. Documentation can be uploaded and shared in a student's profile for use by both parents and teachers. https://www.freshgrade.com

Twitter is used by many teachers as a way to capture the learning that is taking place in their classrooms to share with parents and the online community. Using Twitter is a great way to connect with inquiry teachers across the world and see how pedagogical documentation is used to support inquiry assessment. https://twitter.com

It is important to note that you should always check with the privacy policy of your board or district as there may be conditions to the ownership of material on different apps. When in doubt, consult with your administrator or board technology experts.

Documentation is captured and gathered during the initial stage of inquiry assessment. Once the documentation is captured and triangulated with multiple examples, you can begin the interpretation.

During the interpretation stage, we consider what the documentation is telling us about the learner, our instructional practice and how we can offer support. This interpretation stage should ideally be completed with colleagues to offer multiple perspectives on the documentation.

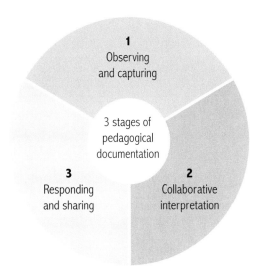

FIGURE 2.15 Pedagogical documentation isn't just about capturing evidence of learning. It involves interpretation and sharing of evidence to improve learning.

TEACHER QUERIES

I take lots of images of student work; aren't I already doing pedagogical documentation?

This is a question we receive frequently. In many spaces, teachers and students are already documenting. Capturing images or videos of student work is a component of pedagogical documentation; however, it is just the first step in the process.

Pedagogical documentation is the process in which we capture, gather, analyze, reflect and make pedagogical moves to support student learning. This shifts documentation beyond the act of simply capturing student learning to one of pedagogy, where the learning is revealed through the documentation and the educator becomes a co-learner with students and colleagues. When we engage in pedagogical documentation, we are engaging in the process of examining and responding to the learning. The educator's pedagogical decisions, the students' voice and their role in their learning interplay in the dynamic process of learning and teaching.

If you are capturing images of student work and are interested in exploring pedagogical documentation, consider spending some time analyzing your triangulated evidence of learning. These guiding questions can help you begin to analyze your documentation:

1. How might this evidence be useful?
2. What patterns or items of interest do we notice from this evidence?
3. What are the limitations of this evidence and what further questions emerge?
4. Based on this documentation, what are the implications for future learning for this student or for our teaching?

Share your documentation with students to hear their perspectives. Having a colleague offer their perspective will also give you an alternative perspective of the learner and their learning. We have included Reproducible 2I, *A protocol for analysis of pedagogical documentation* to support your analysis of student work.

FIGURE 2.16
Reproducible 2I, p. RE15.

With our interpretation of the documentation we consider how we can respond to the documentation and share it. We can also consider what supports we will offer for the learner and how the information can support our assessment of inquiry and professional learning. Students should be invited to be partners in the process of pedagogical documentation and be provided opportunities to capture, select, interpret, respond to and share their learning. This assessment as learning is a powerful tool for developing ownership of their learning and moving an inquiry and dispositions along.

CAPACITY
How can you improve your capacity to manage data for pedagogical documentation?

Managing the data

Gathering documentation to engage in pedagogical documentation can result in large collections of evidence or data on each learner. It is recommended that you develop a plan to ensure you gather evidence that best represents your students over a period of time. Your organization could be as simple as a class list recording sheet where you record observations, or a digital portfolio for each student that holds your assessment data. To build upon the assessment partnership, you may also consider digital student portfolios that you use with students to highlight their learning. The table below offers a few important documentation tips.

Documentation tips	
Take detailed notes	Record the date, time of day, and context in which the image or video was taken. Your notes can be kept in a specific notebook or file, or you can simply jot down who you documented into your day plan book. This attention to detail will help you down the road when you engage in the analysis.
Keep your videos short	Try to keep your video recordings around one minute in length. If you are capturing in the moment of learning, stop after one minute and then start recording again. This will give you smaller videos to work with when you are reviewing your documentation. Long recordings can result in a large digital file and will quickly use up your storage.
Organize your data	Plan your organization strategy in advance. Will you be uploading images and storing them by date, or will you be saving them within student portfolios?
Keep it anonymous	Privacy is a concern when capturing images of students' learning. Try to avoid identifiable features or names of students. Refer to your board or district's policy on capturing images of students.

FIGURE 2.17 The more documentation you do, the easier it will become.

Using pedagogical documentation to determine next steps

Naomi, a grade 7 teacher, and her students have been working on a science unit on life systems and their interactions in the environment. As a Minds On task for their inquiry, she had students develop a concept map on ecosystems. Students were asked to select a central concept and make connections to the other terms provided. Naomi intended to use this task to get students thinking about ecosystems and any questions they may have. She captured some images of students' work to help guide her pedagogical moves on how to support students' development of an inquiry question. The criteria Naomi has in mind are framed in student-friendly language:

Conversation with Student Group A

Naomi: "Explain to me your understanding of the concept you selected."

Student J: "We chose the sun as our central concept. At first we identified what the sun impacts but then realized that the sun is not impacted by anything else. So we then began trying to figure out how everything else needs the sun."

Naomi: "I see you have identified some interconnected relationships. Can you tell me how you identified these?"

Student R: "Once we had made the connections to the sun, we thought about how plants, water, sunlight, soil and animals use the sun. For example, once we saw that plants need to use the sun to grow, they also need soil and water."

Student J: "They also make air that animals use to breathe."

Naomi uses three prompts from the protocol for pedagogical documentation analysis to guide her in determining her students' prior knowledge on ecosystems and identifying her next steps in supporting their learning and guiding her instruction.

What does the documentation suggest about the learner's thinking?

Naomi: "Students can identify some of the relationships between the abiotic and biotic elements of an ecosystem. It appears that group B's image is more linear in the connections whereas in group A's image, students articulate the interconnectedness of the biotic and abiotic elements. In the evidence, groups A and B appear to make vague connections initially and then the connections become more specific as they engage deeper in the task. This is particularly evident in the conversation I had with the students."

What are some questions I have?

Naomi: "When students first began this task they seemed hesitant to expand beyond a linear approach to the ecosystems. Did they initially interpret the instructions as a linear process versus the interrelated nature of the concept? They appeared to be hesitant of breaking a rule or doing something they perceive as wrong. Once they had confirmation that they could expand beyond their initial concept, they began working without limitations and expanded upon their initial concept."

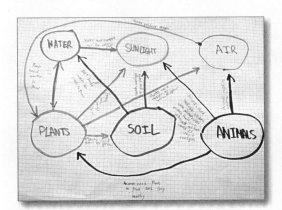

FIGURE 2.18 Student group A's concept map.

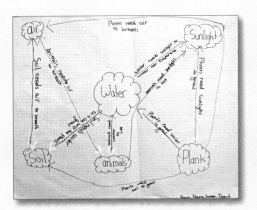

FIGURE 2.19 Student group B's concept map.

continued

How might this information be used to plan for learning?

Naomi: "This task gave students an opportunity to share their prior knowledge and identify relationships between biotic and abiotic components of an ecosystem. Many students identified a linear approach and I will use this as a springboard for discussions on the interconnected nature of ecosystems, as well as from a cross-curricular perspective on other inquiries. I am considering how I can use a concept map to represent interconnectedness among other topics and curriculum and how I can support students in making those big connections. As we move further into our inquiry, I would like students to start exploring ecosystems and making connections to real life."

Naomi's next steps for her unit include supporting students in developing an inquiry question. Her initial task with her documentation has given her a baseline of student understanding and can be used as an assessment as learning tool for students as they reflect back on their learning throughout the inquiry.

THINQ

- How does Naomi's documentation provide her with evidence of student thinking?
- What might the next steps be for the learners?
- What are the limitations to her documentation?

INQUIRY IN ACTION

What if a student is documented in a less than positive light?

Amber had been teaching through inquiry for the past year:

"This year I decided to have students use devices to capture, save and share their learning in digital portfolios. Recently, when I noticed a student filming a peer falling off their chair, I immediately reminded them that they were documenting for assessment and that this was not appropriate or relevant to their learning. I thought the situation was resolved until I found the video posted on our Google Classroom site. This situation got me thinking about how I need to explicitly outline guidelines for documenting others. As a class we discussed why we were documenting and what our documentation represented. We explored respectful documentation, who decides what to share and how we need to have permission when showing someone in a less than positive light. This helped us explore the ideas of ethics in documentation and the role of students, peers and teachers in being respectful of all."

Some things to consider are: making sure that students and parents are aware of why and what you are documenting, allowing students to be involved in the selection of documentation, and a respect for privacy and how you share documentation.

As you review your documentation, we encourage you to consider these guiding ethical questions on pedagogical documentation:

- How do I represent all students in ways that are ethical and respectful?
- How do I decide which image(s) represent learning?
- What should I do when I select images that may show a student in a negative light?
- If I represent a student's difficulties solving a problem, will this be helpful for their learning?

Questions adapted from "Pedagogical Documentation Revisited," 2015.

Communicating with parents

Inquiry-based learning looks very different from the types of classrooms our students' parents may have experienced. Building parental support for an inquiry-based classroom is crucial. Classroom communication should celebrate and clarify what deep learning looks like. Having students articulate their learning in the communications will help parents understand the benefits of inquiry-based learning and alleviate fears and misconceptions. Using classroom blogs or other social media platforms to share examples of student artifacts or quotes resulting from their inquiries will validate the learning and help parents appreciate and support what may be seen as a new type of learning. When communicating with parents, use clear and jargon-less language to help reduce any apprehensions.

Evaluation

Assessment of learning, summative assessment or evaluation is an opportunity for a learner to show their best work at the end point in their learning. This end point in learning is determined by the curriculum or standards and typically comes at the end of an inquiry, unit or problem. Usually, after students have had multiple opportunities to explore the inquiry, skill, concept, problem or disposition, the evaluation is given to see if the student has met the curriculum standard.

Sample parental communication

Parent communications should celebrate and clarify the student's learning using little jargon.

In this sample communication, you will see how Eric's strengths as an inquiry learner are the focus. These strengths are expressed through observations of his understanding and application of content knowledge, his use of skills (inquiry skills and other skills) and his ability to set personal goals for his own learning. This communication will clearly articulate to parents what Eric is learning as well as what his next steps are.

"Eric wants to know more about the balance between environmental stewardship and human needs and wants. He asks important, relevant and deep questions on the environment. He is motivated to answer his question, 'What is my personal responsibility to the environment?' He understands stewardship and the environmental implications, such as individual and societal needs and wants, and the impact on climate change. He sets goals for his learning after reflecting on his challenges (procrastination and selection of sources) and successes (persevering and organization of his notes). He applied his learning to a creative presentation entitled 'Meeting our needs while taking care of the environment.' He worked collaboratively with his group to communicate ideas and conclusions. He encouraged others to become curious and interested in environmental stewardship."

FIGURE 2.20 A sample of a parent communication sharing the results of an inquiry learning unit to parents.

Evaluations should be a given as a repeat performance when students have had an opportunity to practice the standard and receive and utilize feedback. It should not involve a new skill, new understanding, new task, or new criteria of quality. They should not be more complex or carry an additional layer of difficulty that is new to the learners.

We understand that the demands of report cards and marking can make you feel pressured to evaluate frequently; however, we advise holding off on evaluation for as long as possible. A teacher who regularly documents assessment evidence and triangulates their data will have more than enough data on how the student is learning before having to quantify the evidence into a mark against a curriculum standard. In the following chapters on *Wondering and questioning, Investigating and exploring* and *Making sense*, we have provided practical ideas to support assessment and evaluation in each inquiry phase.

Planning

We encourage you to work collaboratively with colleagues to create, implement and revise an inquiry assessment plan. This provides opportunities to professionally reflect on the inquiry question, skills and dispositions you are addressing. An inquiry assessment plan is an outline of your learning intentions based upon your key questions and standards. Work collaboratively to develop answers to these questions. The route of learning in your space may differ from your colleagues'; however, the collaborative planning of key questions will allow you to have a common ground to bring you to the same point.

TEACHER QUERIES

Shouldn't students know the content and have the skills before beginning an inquiry?

At times we are asked to weigh in with an opinion on whether the "how," or the process with which a student applies inquiry skills and dispositions, is more important that the "what," or the specific content knowledge that is required in the inquiry.

This age-old "content versus skills" debate is unhelpful. Inquiry learning is a critical assessment and application of what is already known about a topic, synthesized in new ways to build new knowledge to answer a question or problem. Teachers who claim they must wait until students "know the content" before conducting an inquiry are confused about what inquiry learning is. Teachers who claim that content knowledge is not important to an inquiry are also confused about what inquiry learning is.

Another sticking point for teachers in inquiry learning is the desire to have students master inquiry skills before entering into an inquiry learning unit. This is an impossible aim because the development of inquiry skills is ongoing. Moreover, all learners continue to further develop their inquiry skills despite their years of experience and expertise. As outlined in Chapter 1, inquiry learning is constructivist; the learner is "doing" science, "doing" math and "doing" history in a developmentally-appropriate way. The learner is not a passive witness watching the teacher "talking about" the subject or topic or memorizing information.

The final sticky point of inquiry assessment involves the timing of assessment. Assessment practices of the past were typically "add-ons" at certain points, usually the "end" of a unit of study. Now we view assessment not as events, but as everyday classroom experiences where we show what we know, what we can do, look for advice and feedback, and provide the same for ourselves and our peers.

We have included some questions in Figure 2.21, "Key questions when creating an inquiry assessment plan," to provide you with a starting point in your conversations with colleagues when planning a unit of inquiry. The inquiry assessment plan should be considered a working document and referred to and adjusted as your inquiry unfolds. Keep your plan simple as too many goals, skills or criteria along with too much content will make your interpretation of evidence daunting and confuse your students. Even the most sophisticated of learners do not require their inquiry assessment plan to be filled with more; you would simply expect a higher standard of quality.

THINQ

- How might your school explain to families why inquiry-based learning is important in today's world, and how it can be meaningfully assessed and evaluated?

- What strategies will you use to ensure you are using balanced assessment when gathering, interpreting and evaluating evidence of learning?

- In what ways could you incorporate pedagogical documentation into your assessment for and as learning? How could you engage students?

- What would a reasonable, manageable and valid evaluation of an inquiry entail?

- In what ways could you make the demonstration of quality inquiry skills the most important part of a culminating evaluation?

Key questions when creating an inquiry assessment plan

- How will I get to know my students so that inquiry activities will be purposeful and meaningful to them?

- How can I stretch and extend my students' curiosity and interests in terms of curricular topics and subjects?

- What is the real question or fundamental problem of the inquiry?

- What is the goal of this inquiry (e.g., consider key concepts, inquiry skills, inquiry dispositions, supporting content or corresponding curriculum expectations)?

- How will I sustain student curiosity and interest, voice and choice, diversity and originality?

- What opportunities will I provide for practice and feedback?

- What do I predict may be the areas of greatest student support?

- What are key misconceptions and preconceptions about this concept, topic, phenomenon or process?

- What are the criteria of quality for this inquiry?

- How will I support each student's learning during this inquiry?

- What quality evidence will I gather of student learning for this inquiry?

- How (and when) will I judge student achievement of this inquiry?

FIGURE 2.21 You can use these questions as a starting point for planning an inquiry unit.

Revisit and reflect

Throughout this chapter, assessment and inquiry learning were interwoven. We connected the six essential inquiry abilities as a way to anchor your assessment planning and communication with students.

The overlaying assumptions of the chapter were:

- assessment must be multi-faceted;

- assessment improves both teaching and learning;

- inquiry is a dynamic process where learners assess themselves and each other on an ongoing basis;

- the phases of inquiry assessment (gather, interpret and respond) are dynamic and bring forward student voice and educator responsiveness to the learner; and

- pedagogical documentation can engage the learner and inform the teacher by supporting inquiry assessment.

We explored how to engage students as partners in assessment as well as how pedagogical documentation can support and enhance students' voices, learning and experiences. When all learners can recognize and respond in the moment to the learning taking place during an inquiry, that is what inquiry assessment is all about.

THINQ

- How do the quotes at the beginning of the chapter confirm or challenge your experience with assessment?

- What type of assessment evidence do you gather from your students? Do you feel you have balanced evidence from triangulated sources?

- How might you strengthen student self-assessment of inquiry dispositions?

- In what ways could you make your students partners in inquiry assessment?

- Complete Reproducible 2J, *Teacher checklist: Purposeful planning for inquiry* to further your thinking on effective assessment planning.

BIG IDEAS

2.1 At the heart of assessment are teachers and students are asking, "How are we doing?"

2.2 Curriculum should be seen not as the end, but as the means to engage students in rich learning activities.

2.3 Students should be our assessment partners.

2.4 Inquiry assessment involves gathering, interpreting and responding to evidence of a student's inquiry skills and dispositions.

FIGURE 2.22 Reproducible 2J, p. RE16.

Chapter 3

WONDERING AND QUESTIONING:
The essence of inquiry

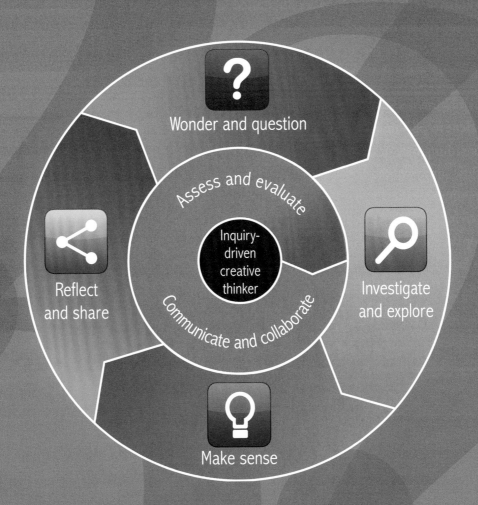

3.1 How can I create a climate of wonder?

Inquiry begins with wonder. When wonder is activated, parts of our brain that hold memory, motivation and reward light up. So when wonder is at work, students' brains are attuned to learning. They become self-engaged and focused. Questions arise. Imagination and critical thought transpire. We believe that our job as educators is to create a climate of wonder by promoting curiosity.

Wonder activities

To ignite learning, we must spark interest. So, how can we kindle wonder and engage our intermediate learners in the inquiry process? Provocations, or wonder activities, which originate from the Reggio Emilia approach, are short activities designed to provoke learners' inherent curiosity. While provocations are often used in preschool and kindergarten, our classroom experience shows us that adapting this approach is also effective in the intermediate grades as life's curiosities engage learners and make them think about the meaning of life.

Wonder activities involve some type of interaction, such as student to material, student to peer or student to media. Wonder activities may introduce something new or cause students to look at something in a new way. While some wonder activities may cause amazement, such as a science experiment, others may trigger outrage, like a real-life story of injustice. Activities that elicit a strong emotional reaction (e.g., "That's so unfair!") or relate to their own experiences and likes tend to engage intermediate learners.

Wonder activities should include time for students to generate questions and have meaningful discussions with their peers. Through interaction, learners will notice that their peers have different emotional responses to various stimuli. They will also recognize that their classmates have distinct knowledge to share. Wonder activities can promote collaborative thinking and critical discussion.

BIG IDEA

Wonder is at the heart of all learning.

COMMITMENT

How willing are you to carve out time for wonder activities and questioning?

CONTEXT

What is the role of wonder in your classroom?

FOOD FOR THOUGHT

"Open your eyes to the beauty around you, open your mind to the wonders of life, open your heart to those who love you, and always be true to yourself."
Maya Angelou

Different wonder activities may create varying degrees of curiosity, depending on the needs, interests and backgrounds of the learners. Engagement will differ from class to class and person to person. The time spent on a wonder activity may vary depending on how much interest it sparks. The following wonder activities can be used to initiate wonder and curiosity in the intermediate classroom. You may wish to supplement a wonder activity with Reproducible 3A, *Student exploration: I see, I think, I wonder, I feel.*

During a wonder activity, the teacher should observe and listen to learners, taking note of what interests them. Using observations of what grabs their attention to plan further lessons is sometimes referred to as the emergent curriculum. Knowing what interests and engages your intermediate learners will help you plan future guided inquiries.

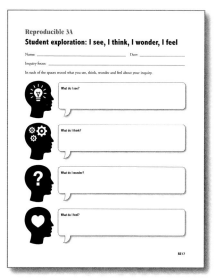

FIGURE 3.1 Reproducible 3A, p. RE17.

CONVICTION
To what extent does the Reggio Emilia approach resonate with you?

CONTEXT
What kinds of wonder activities would appeal to the learners in your classroom?

TEACHER QUERIES

What is the Reggio Emilia approach?

In the Reggio Emilia approach, it is believed that all learners have a deep, innate curiosity and a desire to make sense of the world around them, and that this drives learning. Key aspects include:

1. The learner is an active participant in creating his or her own knowledge.
2. The role of the teacher is to facilitate independent and collaborative discovery and expression.
3. The environment speaks. The classroom is the third teacher.
4. Teachers document and reflect on student thinking and learning.
5. The Reggio Emilia approach is similar to, and complements, an inquiry learning approach.

- **Set out various artifacts** (e.g., an old rotary dial phone or early cell phone, an audio cassette or CD, a gaming console or cartridge from the 1980s or 1990s).
- **Post a tweet, snap, Instagram post or meme** that went viral.
- **Lay out an arrangement of buttons** with different sayings or captions on them and have students choose a button to wear.
- **Display a range of nature photographs or actual items** that showcase the Fibonacci series at work, such as pinecones, pineapples, snail shells or other mollusks with a chambered shell, flowers, sunflower seedheads, etc.
- **Put emojis on cards** and set the cards out in the middle of the tables.
- **Show YouTube clips** where famous people are having an online argument or sharing polar perspectives on a hot topic or current event.
- **Post a news article** about a current social injustice or problem in the news.
- **Look at protest banners** from protests and rallies (e.g., Black Lives Matter) from current and historical times.
- **Juxtapose opposing photographs** (e.g., a child playing in a sprinkler in Canada contrasted with a child carrying a jug of water on her head in a developing nation; or an ad for the latest shoe contrasted with a photo of children working in a factory).
- **Show different kinds of artworks** (e.g., historical painting, abstract, graffiti art, sculpture, art made out of unusual materials, such as art made from marine debris/garbage, etc.).
- **Have students make a list of ten words** that they think are recent additions to the English language, or provide a list of slang words from previous decades (e.g., bee's knees, Moll, Girl Friday, I'll be a monkey's uncle, groovy, The Man, gnarly, preppy, wicked, diss, phat, peeps, word, sick, snake, cheesed, etc.) and have them discuss the possible meanings.
- **Set out trading cards** of various male, female and transgendered sports stars that include statistics such as income.
- **Provide the lyrics of a provocative, popular contemporary song or rap** and have students question the overt and covert messages.
- **Share a law or historical fact** that highlights a social injustice in Canada or a global inequity.
- **Tell a personal family story** in which you model curiosity and questioning (e.g., I wonder why my grandma never went to school). Ask students who feel comfortable to do the same.
- **Display photographs of unusual signs** such as a "no Pokémon and driving" sign beside photographs of people injured playing Pokémon Go.
- **Reveal a hoax that many people believed,** such as using microwaves to charge cell phones or the *War of the Worlds* radio broadcast.
- **Show very short video clips or photographs of coming-of-age ceremonies** from a range of cultures (e.g., quinceañera, bar or bat mitzvah, Tamil puberty ceremony, Brazilian bullet ant initiation, and Chinese, Ethiopian, Kenyan or Inuit coming-of-age traditions).
- **Watch a trailer for a new action movie,** coming-of-age story or whatever types of films your students are talking about. The Teen Choice Awards, The Global Goals Festival or other festivals for young adults and adolescents may offer provocations.
- **Conduct a science experiment** and allow time for speculation before, during and after.
- **Put out microscopes** with unusual slides.
- **Play different types of music** with unfamiliar instruments from various cultures.
- **Post a historical political comic** or an old-fashioned wanted poster.
- **Have students type the words who, what, where, when, why and how into their browser's search bar.** Have them see what the browser predicts they will ask and compare it to other students and other browsers. Also look up some trending searches.
- **Provide a list of common Internet abbreviations** (e.g., lol, brb, omg, ttyl, btw) and contrast it with a short friendly letter or postcard written 100 or 200 years ago.
- **Go for a nature walk** and observe natural phenomena with magnifying glasses. If near a river, go for a riverwalk with nets and catch local specimens, such as crayfish.
- **Walk around the neighbourhood.** Have students take photographs of whatever grabs their attention (e.g., an architectural detail, an ad, a piece of graffiti, litter, a car, etc.)
- **Provide spectacular photographs** for discussion and questioning (e.g., award-winning *National Geographic* photographs).
- **Make a curiosity corner** where students can post articles or pictures that intrigue them.

FIGURE 3.2 These wonder activities are designed as springboards to captivate and engage learners.

From wondering to questioning

Once curiosity is ignited, it is time to shift from wondering to questioning. Learners may be curious about a topic, but may not know how to pose questions about it. As teachers, we should model curiosity, as well as what good questioning looks like. Questioning games are another fun and social way to acclimatize students to a questioning environment.

INQUIRY FOR ALL

Questioning games

Twenty Questions

Have students bring in an item of significance and place it in a mystery bag or box. The other students get to ask 20 questions about it and then try to guess what's inside the bag/box. There are also 20 Q apps or online games in which students think of or look at an object and the computer gets to ask the student 20 questions before identifying the item.

Magic 8 Ball

There was a toy invented in the 1950s that was like a fortune-teller's ball. You ask it a question, and it gives you a reply. There are many Magic 8 Ball apps students can explore to engage questioning.

Why/What if/How?

Introduce an interesting and relevant problem. Give students two minutes to come up with as many questions that start with "why," "what if" or "how" as they can.

Dice Game

Have students work in groups and give each group two dice. On the first die, assign each digit a question starter (e.g., 1 = who, 2 = what, 3 = where, 4 = when, 5 = why, 6 = how). On the second die, assign each digit a topic, which can be generated by the students, depending on their interests (e.g., friendship, a sport, a popular singer, a brand, a video/computer game, etc.). Students take turns rolling the two dice and have to create a question using the question prompt and the topic. Questioning or thinking dice can be bought at a teachers' store or online. Reproducible 3B may also be used to stimulate questioning after a reading or activity.

FIGURE 3.3
Reproducible 3B, p. RE18.

Best Question

Write some popular topics or current events on cards. The "judge" selects a card. Other students in the group have one minute to jot down a question about that topic and pass their question on a card upside down to the judge. The judge then reads all the questions and assigns a point to the person whose question he or she likes the best. The role of judge rotates.

Would You Rather?

In this game, students pose a dilemma for their peers, offering two choices (e.g., "Would you rather swim with sharks or jump off a cliff?"). Students must justify their choice with reasoning.

Ask an Intelligent Assistant

Students can have fun posing questions to a mobile assistant (e.g., Siri, Cortana, Google Now, Robin, etc.) using mobile devices.

continued

Have You Ever

Learners form a circle of chairs. Each person, except for one, is seated in a chair. The person without a chair is "it" and stands in the middle and says, "Have you ever wondered…" (e.g., "Have you ever wondered why school starts so early?" "Have you ever wondered about dreams?" "Have you ever wondered about racism?"). Students who have wondered about the same topic must get up and switch spots with other learners who have the same wondering. The person who is "it" tries to get a chair so someone else will ask a "have you ever wondered…" question.

Beach Ball Madness

Beach balls with questioning prompts can be bought, or you can make your own by writing question starters on each coloured segment of the beach ball (e.g., Who is, what might, how could, etc.). Toss the ball up and whoever catches it has to make up a question.

Pick Two

Photocopy Reproducible 3C on two different colours of card stock. Students must choose one card from each set and make up a question using the two prompts.

FIGURE 3.4
Reproducible 3C,
p. RE19.

INQUIRY IN ACTION

A wonder activity in grade 7 history

To pique students' interest and curiosity in a grade 7 history unit, the following paintings were shown as a wonder activity. The curriculum learning goal was "to analyze the displacement experienced by various groups in or who came to Canada." Learners completed the framework "I see, I think, I wonder, I feel" and then discussed their reactions in small groups. Here are some questions that arose:

- Who are they?
- Where and why are they going?
- Why do some of the people look sad or scared?
- How would you feel if you had to move somewhere new?

Learners then sorted their questions into closed and open questions. They considered what types of questions they were asking (e.g., "How would you feel if you had to move?" is a connecting question and "Why might they be scared or sad?" involves inferring and evaluating). Next, learners considered whether their questions reflected different points of view. The following questions arose:

- Why did the British take land away from the French? How did the British takeover affect the environment and First Nations?
- Is it ever okay to force someone to move to a new place?
- Who can get rich from taking over the land?
- Who would return a runaway slave?

The teacher followed that up by modelling a range of questioning for different purposes:

- How do the depictions of slavery confirm or conflict with what you already thought about slavery in Canada?
- How might the *filles du roi* feel?
- What happened to the Acadians next?
- What would have happened to Harriet Tubman if she had been caught?
- What social attitudes allow slavery to exist?

- Who are the powerful people in the pictures and who are powerless? How do you know?
- How are these images connected?

The use of photographs as a wonder activity (instead of lecturing about examples of displacement) sparked student interest in a subject that some intermediate learners find boring.

Arrival of the Brides, by Eleanor Fortescue Brickman.
Description: These women, who were sent by the King of France to Quebec in order to marry and populate the colony of New France, are greeted by Intendant Talon and Bishop Laval.

Kamloops Indian Residential School cattle truck.
Description: The Canadian government forcibly removed children from their homes and families and took them to a boarding school, where the goal was to "kill the Indian in the child" and assimilate them into British/European culture.

Expulsion of the Acadians, by Lewis Parker.
Description: French descendants living in Acadia (now Nova Scotia) were forcibly expelled from their homes by the British and sent by ships to other colonies or to France.

Harriet Tubman's Underground Railroad, by Paul Collins.
Description: Harriet Tubman helped set up a network of people known as the Underground Railroad to help slaves escape from the southern USA to freedom in Canada.

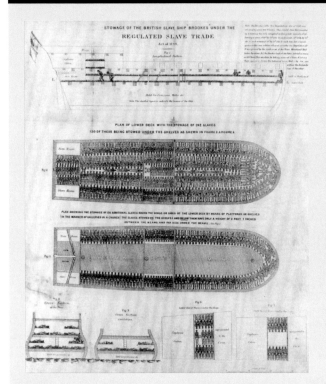

1838 wanted poster for a runaway slave.
Description: Slave owners offered rewards to recapture their slaves who had run away to escape to freedom.

Illustration showing cross sections of the slave ship *Brookes* under the regulated slave trade act of 1788.
Description: From 1600–1834, Canada (New France and British North America) was involved in the transatlantic slave trade. Olivier le Jeune is the first recorded enslaved Black person in Canada. At least 1400 Black people were enslaved in Canada.

THINQ

- How might you use wonder activities or provocations to encourage questioning?

- How can you ensure that wonder activities are culturally relevant and appeal to the diverse interests and backgrounds of learners?

3.2 Why do we start with a question?

Young children are full of wonder and are continually asking questions. Sometimes, when intermediate students have become used to a traditional, transmission style of education, they stop asking questions. In his book *A More Beautiful Question* (2014), Warren Berger concludes that even though children start out asking hundreds of questions a day, questioning "'falls off a cliff" when they begin attending school. Berger reveals that successful people tend to be expert questioners, citing examples of highly successful businesses that are steeped in an inquiry mindset, such as Google, Netflix, IDEO and Airbnb. He suggests that wonder, imagination and "questioning beautifully" lead to game-changing, innovative ideas and solutions.

An inquiry question is a special type of question that drives learning. It is carefully designed to encourage learners to think more deeply and complexly about intellectual ideas. Inquiry questions, sometimes called "framing questions" in curriculum documents, may be used to frame lessons or units of study. They allow us to focus on the big ideas and promote critical thinking. Without questions, there is no inquiry. Questions guide us through our thinking. In their book *Essential Questions* (2013), Jay McTighe and Grant Wiggins state:

- The use of questions signals to your students that inquiry is the goal of learning in your class, and makes it more intellectually engaging.
- The use of questions forces us to clarify and prioritize what is truly important in terms of learning outcomes for our students.

Moreover, the questions students ask can tell us a great deal about them:

- What they know and don't know
- Who they are and what they believe
- Their biases or misconceptions
- Their fears, hopes and concerns
- Their likes, dislikes and interests
- Their culture and experiences

FOOD FOR THOUGHT

"Successful people ask better questions and, as a result, get better answers."

Tony Robbins

STUDENT VOICE

"At first I thought asking questions was pointless, but by the end of my inquiry, my mind changed. I realized that the question I asked myself helped me focus. It made me stick to the point I was trying to learn without getting side-tracked, and it gave me a purpose for reading."

Aiden, Grade 8 student

"In the beginning I didn't have any questions because I felt like my teacher is the one who knows the curriculum and knows what I am supposed to be learning. I thought she is the one who knows what's best for me. She said we can learn about anything, so I started memorizing some grammar rules because my lowest mark is English. Then my teacher suggested to read about something more relevant to the world, and I started to read about ISIS, so I came up with a lot of questions about that. Then I got more curious about it."

Chris, Grade 7 student

Inquiry phase	Types of questions
Wondering and questioning	What am I interested in? What do I need to know? What do I already know and believe?
Investigate and explore	Is the source credible? Whose perspective is represented? Who is speaking? Is it biased? Do I have all the information I need to carefully weigh the evidence?
Making sense	What causes what? What connections can I make? What conclusions can be drawn? How might things be different? Why does it matter? Who should care?
Reflect and share	What have I learned? How have I learned it? How do I know what I know? How can I share this with an authentic audience in a meaningful way?

FIGURE 3.5 Questioning is the first phase of the inquiry cycle, but questioning continues throughout the entire cycle.

THINQ

- How will you create classroom conditions, expectations and group norms that foster curiosity, respect, empathy and open-mindedness?

- How will you encourage a climate of risk-taking, so that students feel comfortable with asking questions?

- How can you help students to become skilled questioners?

- How do the Student Voice examples in this chapter inform your thinking about how students experience inquiry learning?

Some students may feel uncomfortable with questioning. In some cultures, questioning may be seen as rude or disrespectful. Other learners may feel like asking questions makes them look "stupid" or fear they will be laughed at if their question isn't good enough. Sometimes students have simply gotten used to the teacher asking questions or giving answers, so that questioning feels unfamiliar and risky. Learners may come to us believing that the teacher's job is to provide information. We believe that our role as educators is to create classroom conditions that permit open-mindedness and risk-taking, as well as respect for each other. Have conversations with students, parents and caregivers about the value of questioning and its role and purpose in creating an environment in which learners are required to think for themselves.

3.3 What makes a good inquiry question?

A good inquiry question is open-ended, with no right or wrong answer. It cannot be answered by simply regurgitating information. It involves taking a stand and using evidence to support the argument. A question is effective if: (1) it can be revisited over time; and (2) our answer to it will evolve as we learn more.

Funnelling questions

If students tend to ask questions that are too narrow or too specific, you may wish to do some funnelling activities in partners. Funnelling can begin with a narrow question that grows wider, or it can begin as an open-ended question that becomes narrower. Learners can practice their honing skills or work on being more open-ended. Read the following student conversations and consider how you might use funnelling to help students develop their questioning skills.

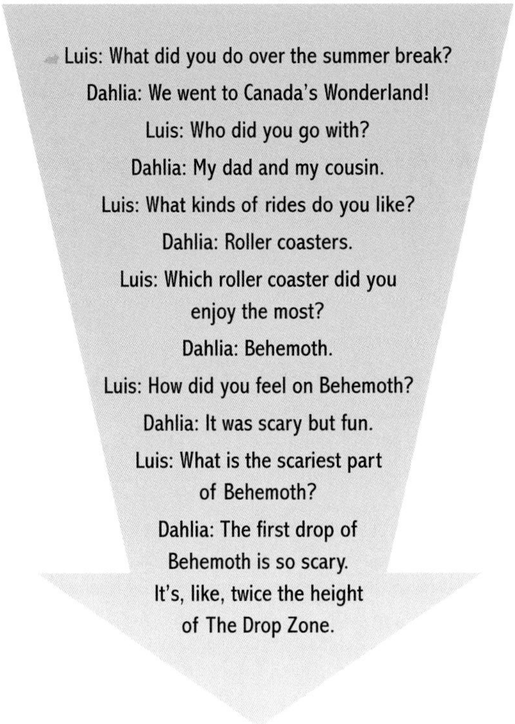

> **BIG IDEA**
> A good inquiry question is an invitation to think. It is open-ended and requires support or a justification to be answered.

> **CONVICTION**
> How convinced are you that a good question is an invitation to think?

Luis: What did you do over the summer break?

Dahlia: We went to Canada's Wonderland!

Luis: Who did you go with?

Dahlia: My dad and my cousin.

Luis: What kinds of rides do you like?

Dahlia: Roller coasters.

Luis: Which roller coaster did you enjoy the most?

Dahlia: Behemoth.

Luis: How did you feel on Behemoth?

Dahlia: It was scary but fun.

Luis: What is the scariest part of Behemoth?

Dahlia: The first drop of Behemoth is so scary. It's, like, twice the height of The Drop Zone.

FIGURE 3.6 Funnelling from open to narrow can help students learn to focus in on something specific.

Sarah: What did you eat for lunch?

Lashaun: A bag of chips and a pop.

Sarah: Do you think that was a healthy lunch?

Lashaun: Not really, but I don't care.

Sarah: Why don't you care about what you eat?

Lashaun: Because it doesn't really matter.

Sarah: How might what you eat today affect you in the future?

FIGURE 3.7 Funnelling from narrow to open can help students create more open-ended questions.

What is your favourite song?

What genre is that?

Why do you like that genre or musical style?

How does this genre influence you?

How might music affect and reflect one's culture and identity?

FIGURE 3.8 This sample line of questioning moves from closed to open questions. What line of funnelling questions could you use in the subjects that you teach?

An effective inquiry question...	
1 ... is an invitation to think (not recall, summarize or detail).	**2** ... comes from genuine curiosity and/or confusion about the world.
3 ... makes you think about something in a way you haven't before.	**4** ... invites both deep thinking and deep feelings.
5 ... leads to more good questions.	**6** ... asks you to think about the essential ideas in a discipline.

FIGURE 3.9 The most effective inquiry questions share common qualities that make them exciting, provocative and intellectually challenging.

Types of questions

Studies show that teachers tend to ask students factual questions. In an inquiry classroom, our goal is to move towards asking more open-ended questions, and model how to create open-ended questions.

Types of questions			
Factual	**Convergent**	**Divergent**	**Evaluative**
Factual questions involve recall, identification and memorization of facts, and simple yes-or-no answers. They usually require a short sentence to answer.	Convergent questions have a small range of possible answers. They tend to involve comprehension, analysis, application and interpretation. Students may need to summarize information or explain an idea.	Divergent questions require logical projections, inference, imagination, creation, conjecture and synthesis.	Evaluative questions depend on weighing multiple perspectives and drawing conclusions. These questions require comparison, generalization, problem-solving, higher order thinking and affective thinking.
Bloom's Taxonomy • Remember (Knowledge)	Bloom's Taxonomy • Understand • Comprehend • Apply	Bloom's Taxonomy • Analyze • Create	Bloom's Taxonomy • Evaluate

FIGURE 3.10 This chart shows the relationship between types of questions and Bloom's Taxonomy.

The role of closed questions

An intermediate teacher wants his students to answer the inquiry question "How will we address the issue of marine debris?" (Marine debris, also known as an ocean garbage patch, is a vast floating mound of garbage in the ocean, consisting mainly of plastics and nets.) The learning goals of the unit are cross-curricular, incorporating science, geography and language. It focuses on the big idea that our actions impact the environment (e.g., water, animals, soil). The topic is relevant because marine debris affects students, whether they know it or not, and the question is open-ended.

So, what's the problem? If students do not have background knowledge on the topic, they may not be successful with their inquiry. Here's where teachers can prompt students to start with closed questions, so that they can gain some background knowledge. Here are some example questions that students may ask and find answers to before tackling the main inquiry question:

- What is marine debris?
- Where is marine debris found?
- Who contributes to marine debris?

- Who can help reduce marine debris?
- How does marine debris affect the health of humans and animals?
- Why should I care about marine debris?
- Who is responsible for dealing with this issue?
- How do my actions affect marine debris?
- What actions am I willing to take to address the problem of marine debris?

In this example, one question can lead to the next. As students gain more knowledge, their questioning can begin to widen. A key part of inquiry is shifting from knowledge-based to action-based questions. As you can see in this sample line of thinking, the student moves toward a solution. This is where innovation lies. New ideas and solutions to problems are investigated, but it started with a simple closed question. Towards the end of the inquiry, students can take action and do something, such as clean-up a shoreline, share what they have learned with younger students and family members, write to a fishery, or do a neighbourhood clean-up while raising awareness.

Examples of subject-specific or content-related inquiry questions

Subject-specific inquiry questions should be posted in the classroom and shared with students electronically or in print at the beginning of the unit, so that students can immediately see that they will have to think through the answers, not memorize facts. Inquiry questions can be used throughout a unit of study and then be posed as a final assessment piece and as part of your evaluation. On the next pages are some subject-specific examples of inquiry questions that you may wish to use as a springboard if you are doing a guided inquiry or teacher-directed inquiry. Further examples can generally be found in curriculum documents.

CONVICTION

Do you believe that the role of education is to pose the right question, or to provide the correct information?

FOOD FOR THOUGHT

"Good teaching is more a giving of right questions than a giving of right answers."
Joseph Albers

Literacy/Language Arts

- Who am I? How is identity created?
- How does what I see, read and hear influence me?
- How does the media influence me?
- What is hope?
- To what extent is Canada a free country?
- How can we make a difference in our community?
- What makes a good friend?
- How do different media outlets present the same news story in different ways?
- How does environmental racism impact various Canadians?
- Do all Canadian students have equal opportunities for success?
- How do we build equity?
- How could selfies reflect our social values?
- How might one's online identity be different from their real-world identity?
- Who should own your social media accounts after you've passed on?
- Why might various groups react differently to doctor-assisted death?
- How might men react to be calling "boys"? How might women react to being called "girls"?
- What power is involved in a racial slur?

Mathematics

- Why might a business owner, shipper or distributor need to know the theory of conservation in math?
- How do we use operations with fractions and integers in our daily lives?
- How can we use multiples and factors in the real world?
- How can knowing the area rule for a rectangle help us determine the area of a triangle, parallelogram, trapezoid or circle if we cut and manipulate the paper?
- What is the relationship between perimeter and area, or surface area and volume?
- When do we "do math" in our day-to-day lives?
- How can studying patterns help us understand nature and the universe?
- Why is financial literacy important?
- In a triangle, what is the relationship among side lengths and the squares of side lengths?
- How can we make a reasonable estimate? Why is estimation valuable?
- How can we justify a conjecture?

Science and Technology

- How do biotic and abiotic elements rely on each other?
- How do humans impact ecosystems?
- How do we know what shape or form a structure should take?
- Why is it important for companies to predict what people will want and need in the future?
- How can we design something ergonomically?
- How do substances and mixtures impact the environment?
- How does changing the amount of solute or solvent affect the solution?
- How do oil refineries impact local populations?
- How does knowing particle theory help us understand the world around us?
- What effect does heat have on the environment?
- How might understanding cells help us prevent or cure diseases?
- How do systems maximize human and natural resources?
- What is the relationship between mass, volume and density?
- Why is water important?
- How are technologies impacting water systems?
- Why is water quality different in different regions of Canada and in different countries?

History

- Is history truth or fiction? How do we know what is true?
- Why might primary sources from different perspectives be helpful when studying history?
- What makes someone or something historically significant?
- What does it mean to be Canadian?
- What impact did the fur trade have on various groups in Canada?
- How did people in the past deal with conflict?
- What attitudes allowed slavery to exist?
- What are the lasting effects of colonialism?
- What are the lasting effects of Canada's residential schooling system?
- How have treaties impacted First Nations people?
- How did power shift during the 18th Century?
- Why might the First Nations, French and British have had different perspectives on the Loyalist migration?
- What impact has slavery and the American Revolution had on Canada?
- What's the difference between a hero, a rebel and a traitor?
- Were Louis Riel and Alexander Mackenzie heroes or traitors?
- Is war ever justified?

History (continued)
- How have racialized groups been marginalized in Canada and what efforts have been and are being made to work towards equity?
- What kinds of forces bring about change?
- Is historical change good or bad?
- Why are some people displaced?
- How did different groups react to the creation and expansion of the Dominion of Canada?
- How have the struggles of people in the past affected us today?
- Why is studying history important?

Geography
- How do my actions help or harm the environment?
- How might I reduce my carbon footprint, and why should I care?
- How do we deal with challenges caused by Earth's forces?
- How do humans cause changes in vegetation patterns, landforms and water systems, and how do these changes affect animals and humans?
- How are we addressing our use of natural resources?
- Why should we care about fish, soil or forests?
- What are some of the challenges associated with flow resources?
- How do settlements affect the environment?
- Why should I care about climate change?
- How can we create more sustainable communities?
- How can we balance our needs and wants with environmental sustainability?
- How might my quality of life differ if I lived in different regions of the world?
- What factors affect quality of life and how can we improve quality of life in developing nations?
- How is Canadian identity tied to our natural landscape?
- What criteria should be used to determine Canada's immigration policy?
- How can we deal with conflicts over land use and development?

Dramatic Arts
- How have theatre productions changed over time and across different communities, and what does that tell us about society?
- What value do you think the dramatic arts has in your life and in your community?

Health
- How might one develop a healthy self-concept, and why should one develop a healthy self-concept?
- How can I stand up to bullying and make others feel included?
- Why is a healthy, balanced diet important?
- How could impaired or distracted driving impact someone's life?
- Is technology beneficial or dangerous? Why is communication so important in a relationship?
- Is stress always bad? How can I manage stress?
- What are the advantages and disadvantages of processed meats?
- How can sugar affect me?
- Why might mental illness have a stigma in some communities?

Visual Arts
- How do we know what is beautiful or valuable? Who defines beauty?
- Why might different groups or people interpret works of art differently?
- How does art contribute to culture?
- How can artworks we create make a statement or convey a belief?

Dance
- How can movements communicate ideas? How can motion show emotion?
- How can dance be used to show multiple perspectives?
- What factors influence the evolution of certain dance styles over time?
- How can dance shown in popular media affect our body image?

Music
- How does music unite us or divide us?
- What are the implied messages in the music you listen to?
- How has our national anthem changed and evolved over time? How might it change in the future?
- What is the role of music?

FIGURE 3.11 There are no "right" inquiry questions. What questions could drive learning in the context and community in which you teach?

THINQ

- What open-ended inquiry questions could you use to frame a unit of study?
- To what extent do you see yourself as a provider of knowledge or a questioner?
- How can carefully planned questions improve student thinking?

3.4 How can I help students create their own inquiry questions?

In section 3.3, we provided some sample questions for guided inquiries or teacher-directed inquiries. In this section, we will explore how to help students generate their own questions for an open inquiry. During an open inquiry, students take the lead by developing their own questions and selecting appropriate resources. There is a misconception that inquiry-based learning means that the teacher lets go and takes a back seat. Students are left to "figure things out" on their own. This is not true. Teachers differentiate instruction during open inquiry and provide varying levels of support, depending on the readiness of the students to complete an independent inquiry. During each phase of the inquiry, teachers model how to engage in inquiry, starting by modelling how to create a good question. They may begin an open inquiry cycle by sharing their own interests, curiosities and questions about the world. Teachers can then invite the learners to discuss what they are curious about.

The Q chart, or questioning chart, can be a helpful tool to assist students with starting off their questions. You may find rubrics showing that questions that begin with "who is" or "what did" are scored as a level 1, while questions that begin with "how could" or "why might" are scored as a level 4. However, it is very possible that a deep, higher-order thinking question may begin with "who is," for example, "who is powerful?" On the other hand, it is also possible that a question that begins with "how could" may be a simple, factual or lower-level thinking question. Using the criteria for a good question should help both students and teachers assess the effectiveness of their questions.

BIG IDEA
Students are most engaged when they self-direct their learning. High engagement improves student achievement.

COMMITMENT
To what extent are you and your students ready to do open inquiry? If you are already doing open inquiry, how much time will you commit to open inquiry in your classroom?

CONFIRMATION
How might you share your students' inquiry questions with your colleagues or other authentic audiences?

FOOD FOR THOUGHT

"My mother made me a scientist without ever intending to. Every other Jewish mother in Brooklyn would ask her child after school, 'So? Did you learn anything today?' But not my mother. 'Izzy,' she would say, 'did you ask a good question today?' That difference — asking good questions — made me become a scientist."

Isidor Isaac Rabi

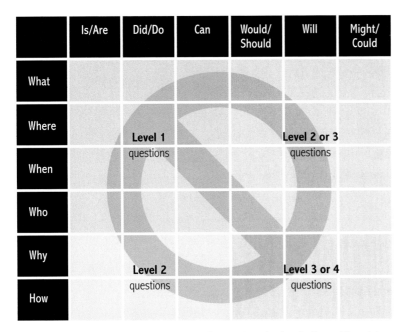

	Is/Are	Did/Do	Can	Would/Should	Will	Might/Could
What						
Where		Level 1			Level 2 or 3	
When		questions			questions	
Who						
Why		Level 2			Level 3 or 4	
How		questions			questions	

FIGURE 3.12 Some models may level questions in the Q chart. We advise against using these models to assess questioning, as both simple and deep questions can occur anywhere on the chart.

	Is/Are	Did/Do	Can	Would/Should	Will	Might/Could
What						
Where		Factual			Predictive	
When		questions			questions	
Who						
Why		Analytical			Application Synthesis	
How		questions			questions	

FIGURE 3.13 This Q chart makes a great anchor chart or visual aid to help students formulate questions throughout the year.

While there are benefits to open inquiry, there are also risks. Sometimes students take a wrong turn or encounter a dead end. As facilitators, our role is to reorient learners in a successful direction or bring them back to a teacher-directed inquiry until they have developed the independent skills necessary for open inquiry.

Another problem that teachers worry about is students getting off-task. If learners are truly curious about and interested in the topic, they should be self-motivated to persevere with the inquiry. If students are getting off-task, consider if it is the question, their readiness, their habits of mind (inquiry dispositions) or lack of engagement in school. Try to talk to students about the issues that affect their own lives and investigate ways to approach these issues. Adolescents can sometimes be egocentric, so learning about issues that affect them personally is a good place to start.

Finally, there is a concern that inquiry takes too long. While it is true that inquiry takes longer than providing students with information, we believe that by doing the work themselves, there will be deep, enduring understanding. Further, in today's information age, it's not necessary for learners to recall facts and information, as knowledge is readily available and rapidly changing. However, students do need to learn how to process information and to develop critical and creative thinking skills.

What are some ways to promote questioning?

After modelling questioning and introducing the Q chart, teachers might use some of the following ideas to get students to develop their questioning skills:

CONFIRMATION
What strategies to promote questioning have worked for you in the past?

- **Read a short story** based on real-life experiences featuring stories of social injustice (e.g., Japanese internment, residential schools, Africville, etc.) and have students create five questions they have about the text.
- **Post your own questions** online, on a social media site, or on chart paper and invite students to add on.
- **Share an online news article** that everyone is talking about and ask students to create five questions about it.
- **Have students keep a questioning journal** throughout the year in which they jot down things that interest them or make them wonder. This could be done using an online notebook, such as OneNote, which allows students to capture voice-to-text, photographs, articles, tweets and more into one notebook.
- Hang a **"graffiti wall"** on which students can write down their wonderings.
- Keep **teen magazines** on hand or provide access to popular, appropriate teen news websites (e.g., Teen Tribune, Newsela) and allow students to choose a news article that interests them. Then ask them to create a list of questions sparked by the news article. Sharing questions using a social media app or interactive classroom platform may engage the intermediate learner.
- Feature a **question of the day** posed by a student. Use assessment as learning to discuss the strengths of the question, as well as ways to reframe or improve it.
- **Create a question continuum** and have students post questions on sticky notes from most closed to most open along the continuum.
- Have students **sort their questions into categories**: factual, convergent, divergent and evaluative. Alternatively, have them sort their questions into two categories: closed and open-ended; or ask students to create their own sorting rules.

Graphic organizers

Graphic organizers can be used to help learners organize their questions. We have provided some reproducibles. Students may also wish to use online mind-map makers (e.g., mindmup.com, bubbl.us, Google Drawings) to brainstorm questions and show how their questions connect and relate.

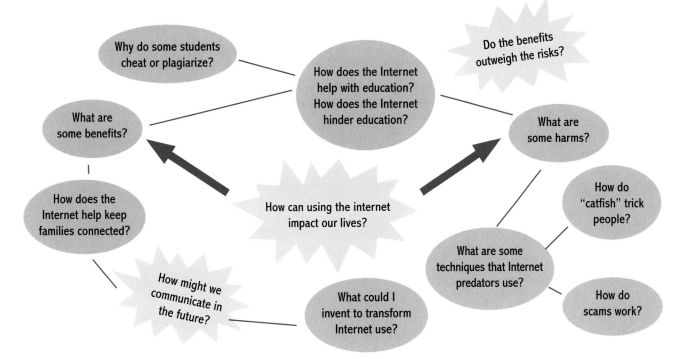

FIGURE 3.14 Students may use online mind-map makers or create a mind map with paper and pencil to record their questioning and show how questions relate to each other.

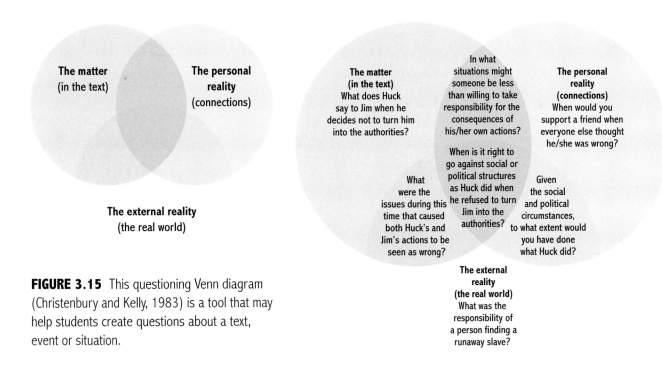

FIGURE 3.15 This questioning Venn diagram (Christenbury and Kelly, 1983) is a tool that may help students create questions about a text, event or situation.

FIGURE 3.16 This example of questioning on *Adventures of Huckleberry Finn* (Christenbury and Kelly, 1983) is provided as an example of types of questions you may wish to pose to your students.

KWHLAQ chart

The KWHLAQ chart can be introduced during the questioning stage of the inquiry process. During this stage of inquiry, learners should complete the first two rows, *Know* and *Want to know*. The other sections of the chart can be completed throughout the inquiry cycle. Using Google Docs, OneNote or another online platform can be a useful way to store and manage the KWHLAQ chart. The KWHLAQ chart should be seen as a "living document" that can be revisited and revised throughout the inquiry cycle. We will revisit the KWHLAQ chart in Chapter 4.

Getting started with open inquiry

Teachers who are new to open inquiry may wish to start off with one Passion Project or have a weekly Genius Hour. A passion project is generally a month spent learning about something that you've always wanted to know how to do. Genius Hour is a set period, such as 40 or 60 minutes per week, dedicated to students learning about what truly inspires them. The rationale is that when students are allowed to work on something that interests them, productivity will increase.

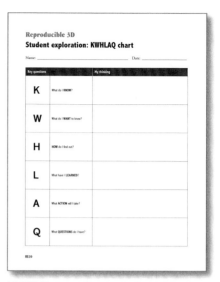

FIGURE 3.17 Reproducible 3D, p. RE20.

INQUIRY IN ACTION

Using short stories as a springboard for questioning

Students were asked to discuss the following questions in small groups:

1. When is the best time to do things?
2. Who is the most important one?
3. What is the right thing to do?

Then the teacher read aloud Jon Muth's *The Three Questions* (adapted from a story by Leo Tolstoy). In the text, Leo the turtle is searching for answers to life's greatest mysteries, but his friends aren't giving him the answers he seeks. At the end, Leo discovers that the answers to his questions

can be found by reflecting on his experiences, and that the answers lie within himself.

After listening to the text, students revisited their answers to see if their thinking had changed. The teacher explained that these philosophical questions require thinking about their beliefs. Learners were then prompted to create five open-ended questions like the ones in the book. The students then discussed their questions in small groups. Each group came up with a list of five intriguing questions to share with the whole class. Following that, each learner was given three stickers to place as votes beside the questions that most interested them. Finally, students reflected on why they chose certain questions and came up with a list of criteria for what makes an effective inquiry question.

Revising open inquiry questions

Intermediate students are interested in increasingly complex and deep issues. Sometimes students have a keen interest in something but need our help to generate questions about the topic or issue. If students have limited experience with questioning or inquiry, they may require support with reframing or revising their inquiry questions.

A leading question suggests or anticipates a certain answer, often a yes or no. A loaded question contains a bias and suggests or implies some fact before the inquiry has begun. Teacher or peer conferencing may help students detect bias in their questioning, as well as learn how to recognize questions with dead ends or simple answers.

How can we help learners create questions that reflect open-mindedness? We don't want them entering the inquiry process with their minds already made up. They need to create questions that allow them to carefully weigh evidence from multiple perspectives. Read the examples below and consider how you might help each student reframe his or her question, so that the learner enters the inquiry without a bias.

FIGURE 3.18 What suggestions would you make to these students to help them create more open-ended, unbiased questions?

Initial inquiry question	Reframed question
Is it true that processed meat is bad for me?	What are the implications of eating processed meats?
Can playing video games make me a better student?	How can video games affect my performance at school?
Why are GMOs bad?	How are GMOs helpful or harmful?
What are the different genres of video games?	How might different genres of video games appeal to different audiences?
Do you agree that we should save the rainforest?	How can we deal with conflict about using rainforest resources?
Is x the best game console/phone/laptop?	What features of a console/phone/laptop might appeal to different consumers?
Do teens like social media site x the best?	What criteria make a social media site more popular than others?
Why do I like celebrity x so much?	How does celebrity x influence me? What makes celebrity x so influential?

THINQ

- Are your students ready for open inquiry?
- How can you move your students toward more open inquiry?
- To what extent do you embrace open inquiry?

3.5 What questions can help students reflect on their thinking?

Students need time and tools to assess their own questioning and critical thinking skills. Success criteria and rubrics for effective questioning may help them self-assess their thinking and planning skills. Teachers should set aside time for conferencing with learners about metacognition, to encourage them to "think about their thinking."

In their work on critical thinking, Paul and Elder (2010) identify eight universal elements of thought that can be used to analyze and improve thinking. Questions based on the eight elements of thought can help your students during an inquiry.

BIG IDEA

Students need time to reflect on their questioning skills.

CONTEXT
Which of the eight elements of thought are most common in your classroom, and which ones would you like to see more of?

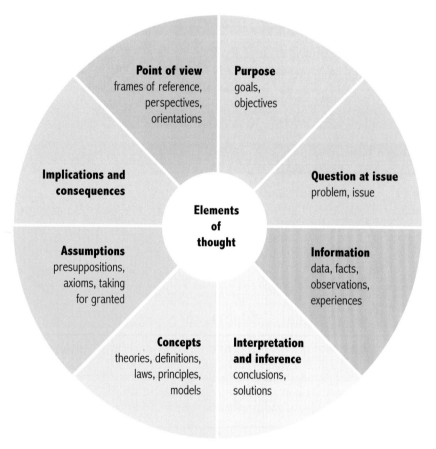

FIGURE 3.19 Learners can use the eight elements of thought to "think about their thinking" and improve it. This tool can be used to help students reflect on what types of questions they have most often and which areas of thinking they should work on.

STUDENT VOICE

"At first my question was, 'How can I become a millionaire?' Then my teacher posted a documentary about the Chemical Valley in Sarnia, and it grabbed my attention. I noticed that the Aamjiwnaang First Nations who live near the chemical industries and oil refineries are getting sick from pollution. So I decided to change my inquiry question. I became more interested in the social justice side of it. I wanted to find out who's behind all of it and how I could help. I changed my question so I could look at more perspectives. I asked, 'How does our need for oil and chemicals impact other communities in Canada, such as the Aamjiwnaang?' I think my questioning skills got better."

Raj, Grade 7 student

3.6 How can I assess questioning?

Teachers may assess learners' questioning skills through conversations, observations and products. A conversation may look like a teacher conference; an observation may include watching learners interact in a group, as well as how they socialize in the halls; and a product may be a digital work or on-paper task. Reproducible 3E, *Assessment planning template: Asks questions* can be used for ongoing assessment for, as and of learning. Reproducible 3F, *Inquiry rubric and self-check: Asks questions* is a single point rubric that students may use for self-assessment or peer-assessment. Using a checklist, such as Reproducible 3G, *Success criteria for a good question*, is a simple tool for students to self-assess whether their inquiry questions meet requirements or expectations for this initial phase of the inquiry learning cycle. To reflect on your own teaching practice, Reproducible 3H, *Teacher checklist: Curiosity and questions in my classroom* is offered.

BIG IDEA

Teachers can help students improve their questioning skills through feedback.

CAPACITY

What tools could help you assess questioning?

CONTEXT

How can you give your students constructive feedback to help them become better questioners?

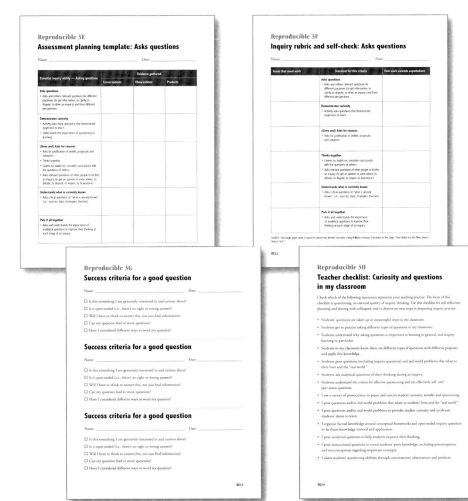

FIGURE 3.20–3.23
Reproducibles 3E, 3F, 3G and 3H, pp. RE21–RE24

Creating and co-creating criteria for an effective inquiry question

You may wish to create or co-create criteria for a good inquiry question with students. If students are new to inquiry, you may need to provide them with some examples of inquiry questions before asking them to identify the criteria.

In John Barell's book *Developing More Curious Minds* (2003), he provides a list of criteria for an effective inquiry question, stating that a good question:

- is an invitation to think (not to recall, summarize or regurgitate a detail).
- comes from genuine curiosity and confusion about the world.
- makes you think about something in a way you never considered before.
- leads to more questions.
- asks you to think critically, creatively, ethically, productively and reflectively about essential ideas in a discipline.

Student-created criteria for a good question	
Initial success criteria	**Revised criteria over time**
1. It is interesting.	1. It appeals to you personally.
2. It is open-ended.	2. It leads to new questions.
3. You have to support it with reasons.	3. It makes you think about your position on an issue in a way that you never thought about before.
	4. You have to try and figure out a solution to answer it.

FIGURE 3.24 Criteria may change over time as students become better questioners.

Student discussion: Providing peer feedback

Janette: What's your inquiry question?

Nareesh: My question is "Where did the Paris attacks take place?"

Janette: That's not an inquiry question. You answered the question *in* the question. The answer is "Paris."

Nareesh: Well, I meant, like, in more detail, like specifically where.

Janette: But that's too easy to answer. All you have to do is Google it and, bam, you're done. You need a question that's more open-ended.

Nareesh: Ummm...how about, why did the Paris attacks take place?

Janette: I think that's better, but you should ask yourself something more general, like how might governments respond to terror attacks; or what effect do terror attacks have on the Muslim community; or how have terror attacks changed our world?

Nareesh: Okay, I'll think about something more open.

THINQ

- What classroom conditions and group norms would need to be in place to allow students to engage in critical feedback with each other about their questioning skills in inquiry?

- How can critical feedback from peers and from the teacher help learners to improve their inquiry questions?

Sharing inquiry questions

You can have students post their inquiry questions on an interactive electronic platform, such as a board-sponsored site. When using Twitter, Snapchat, Instagram or other social media sites to share inquiry ideas, be sure that students have read and complied with your board's media/Internet policy. Also make sure that you have linked your class's social media account to your school's main website. Some possibilities:

- Google Hangouts
- Bubbl.us, Cacoo or other mind-map-making apps
- Twiddla.com or interactive whiteboard apps
- Edmodo, PowerSchool Learning or Google Classroom

Differentiating communication and sharing

Encourage students to use speech-to-text and text-to-speech apps, such as Read&Write Gold to post their questions electronically and to provide peer feedback.

Revisit and reflect

This chapter looked closely at the importance of wonder and curiosity to engage intermediate learners. A classroom culture that encourages open-mindedness and risk-taking fosters wonder. We offered some wonder activities or provocations to spark student interest.

We outlined the importance of creating powerful inquiry questions that can capture and hold student interest and drive their learning forward. We provided tools and examples for helping students distinguish weak or thin questions from strong and powerful ones.

The research shows that guided inquiry, where the question and methods for answering it are provided by the teacher, is an effective place to start. We believe that open inquiry is also effective when it is scaffolded and ongoing feedback is provided, starting with teacher direction on revising the question. Blended inquiry is an approach that combines both student autonomy and teacher direction.

BIG IDEAS

3.1 Wonder is at the heart of all learning.

3.2 Questions drive learning forward.

3.3 A good inquiry question is an invitation to think. It is open-ended and requires support or a justification to be answered.

3.4 Students are most engaged when they self-direct their learning. High engagement improves student achievement.

3.5 Students need time to reflect on their questioning skills.

3.6 Teachers can help students improve their questioning skills through feedback.

THINQ

- What do you think would be the best way to create more wonder in your classroom?

- How has your understanding of what a good inquiry question is changed as a result of this chapter?

- How will you make time in your curriculum and classroom to allow students to ask, reflect on and refine their own inquiry questions?

- Are you ready to place as much emphasis on assessing asking questions as answering questions?

Chapter 4

INVESTIGATING AND EXPLORING:
Finding answers to inquiry questions

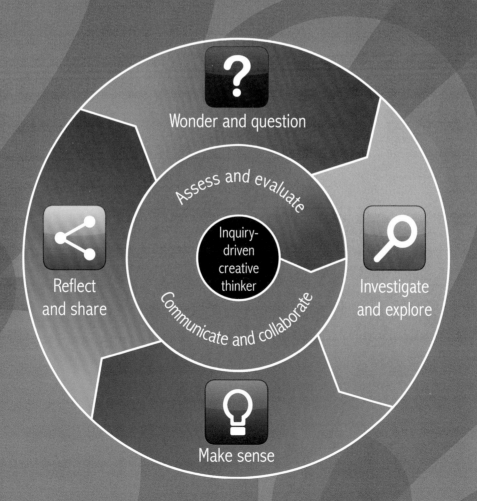

4.1 What are some ways of investigating and exploring?

Now that learners have been provided with or have developed an inquiry question, it is time to explore the issue. An issue can be explored and investigated through observation, experimentation, an activity, a discussion or debate, role play, games, interacting with materials, reading an infographic and many other ways. Like a detective, students can investigate by interviewing others, looking at clues or collaborating with peers. As a first step, students should brainstorm various ways to seek answers, including the use of human resources (e.g., librarian, community member, parent, etc.). Reproducible 4A, *Brainstorming ways to gather evidence* may be used a starting point.

Internet
E-zines   Websites
E-books   Podcasts
Online   Videos
newspapers   Webcasts

People, oral communication
Field trips   Discussions with
Elders   experts
Interviews   Family members
               Friends

Finding answers to our questions

Library, museum or print
Magazines   Graphic novels
Books   Brochures
Newspapers   Documentaries

Objects
Statues   Paintings
Plaques   Photographs

FIGURE 4.1 Learners can brainstorm ways to investigate and explore an issue using a web or mind map.

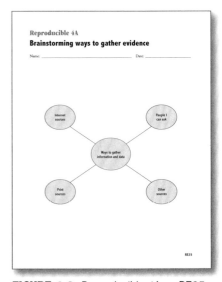

FIGURE 4.2 Reproducible 4A, p. RE25.

A math investigation

A grade 7 teacher posed this question to her students: "Where should we go for a field trip?" The learning goals of the inquiry were to read and interpret data, to represent data in a circle graph, and to solve multi-step number problems arising from real-life situations.

First the learners had to create a list of possible places to visit, along with ways to obtain information and data. Some ideas included:

- Get the phone number of the place and call to ask questions.
- Send the place an email request for information.
- Look on their web page in the *school trips* or *education tab*.
- Do a Google Hangouts call with a neighbouring school to ask them for feedback on trips they've done.
- Read reviews on TripAdvisor or other rating apps.
- Look at brochures, posters and promotional print material received by the school from trip vendors.

Next, they formed criteria to consider when selecting a location. Criteria included:

- Location, distance from school (using map apps), travel costs (read tables, charts)
- Cost of event, divided among participants (including 13% tax)
- Indoor or outdoor
- Permissions: teacher, principal, parents, relationship to the curriculum

After that, learners had to research costs (and weather forecasts for outdoor trips). Each group calculated the cost per student for a particular trip and then presented their findings, providing facts, evidence, data and curriculum links to promote that place as the superior choice.

Finally, students voted on the trip of their choice. The results of the vote were displayed by students in a variety of charts and graphs, including a circle graph and computer-generated charts. The results were shared with parents, teachers and the principal, and a final decision to book the trip was made.

THINQ

- Which types of evidence do your students use most often? Which kinds of evidence might be new to them?
- How can your school or community librarian help you and your students complete an inquiry?

CONVICTION
What kind of evidence is easiest for your students to access? What kind of evidence is harder for them to access?

4.2 How could bias affect the investigating and exploring stage?

Intermediate learners may be inclined to locate evidence that supports their preconceived notions or preexisting beliefs. They may use search terms that defend the conclusion they already have in mind, while overlooking evidence that reflects divergent viewpoints. This is known as confirmation bias. For example, a learner in a health class may wish to answer the question, "How healthy are grains?" If the student already believes that adolescents should eat 6–7 servings of grains per day, she may look to the *Canada Food Guide* to support that belief. She may not consider using search terms such as *wheat belly, grain-free diet, harmful effects of GMO wheat, gluten sensitivity,* etc.

Many intermediate students may think that bias is always a bad thing. A bias is simply a preference in favour of or against something. We can have a bias for or against pickles, for or against school uniforms, or for or against a political candidate. Intermediate learners should be explicitly taught that having a bias means looking at something from a one-sided perspective. Figure 4.3 shows an example of how a learner's point of view could impact their search while answering an inquiry question.

BIG IDEA

Learners should reflect on their assumptions or biases and collect evidence from a variety of perspectives.

FOOD FOR THOUGHT

"Good questions are those that force students to challenge their taken-for-granted assumptions and see their own underlying biases. Oftentimes the answer to a good question is irrelevant — the question is an insight in itself. The only answer to the best question is another good question. And so the best questions send students on rich and meaningful lifelong quests, question after question after question."

Michael Wesch

WORDS MATTER

Preconception: Idea or opinion formed *before* learning about or experiencing something directly.

Misconception: View or idea based on faulty or misinformed thinking.

Bias: Prejudice for or against something, often considered to be in an unfair manner.

Point of view: "Do your actions as a consumer impact climate change?"	Possible impacts on the investigating stage
"My parents say that corporations leave a much larger environmental footprint than individuals, so I'd say no."	Student may overlook information that contradicts her currently held belief.
"I read an article that said climate change research is biased and the Earth goes through natural heating and cooling patterns, so I don't think it matters."	Student may disregard scientific data (e.g., from NASA) during the exploring and investigating stage.
"I don't think so because we don't have a car, and I saw a TV show that said that driving is the main cause of global warming."	Student may be inclined to draw a conclusion before gathering further evidence or exploring other contributors.

FIGURE 4.3 There are many ways in which point of view can impact the exploring and investigating stage of the inquiry.

Before selecting resources, students may complete Reproducible 4B, *Assessing my point of view and assumptions* as a metacognitive exercise in considering how their biases could affect their choice of search terms. Encourage them to keep an open mind and look at the issue from a variety of perspectives before making judgments or drawing a conclusion. Asking learners to consider diverse perspectives is not an attempt to change their minds, but rather an invitation to understand the variety of views people have on issues. Further, without a sufficient array of sources from multiple perspectives, the response to the inquiry will be an opinion, not critical thinking. Students may wish to look at debate sites or discussion forums if experiencing difficulty imagining divergent viewpoints.

When exploring multiple perspectives, students may consider the following questions (adapted from the Ontario Ministry of Education's *Adolescent Literacy Guide* (2012)):

1. What does the author want me to know, think or feel? How do I know this?

2. What view of the world does this source present? How do I know this?

3. What voices, points of view and perspectives are missing from this source, or all of my sources? How significant is this omission?

4. Is this source fair? Why or why not?

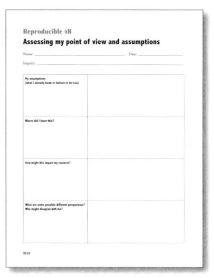

FIGURE 4.4 Reproducible 4B, p. RE26.

COMMITMENT
Are you willing to reflect on and share some of your own misconceptions with students?

CONTEXT
How might your own biases and beliefs affect the sources that you select for students?

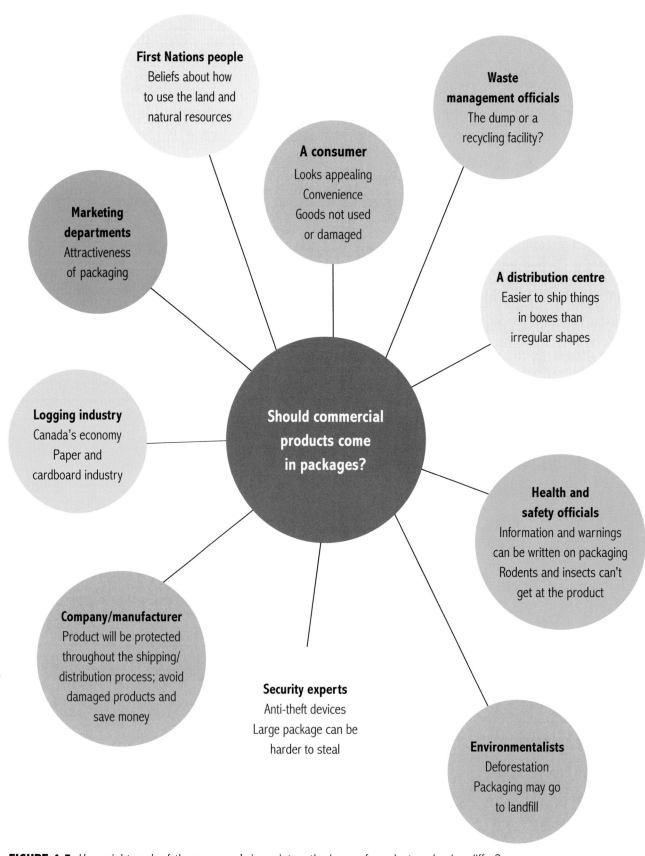

FIGURE 4.5 How might each of these groups' viewpoint on the issue of product packaging differ?

Divergent thinking

Divergent thinking is a creative thought process in which many possible solutions to a problem are explored. Canadian studies show that 98% of four-year-olds could be classified as divergent thinkers, while by age 12 it withers down to 10%. Divergent thinking is like a muscle that needs to be flexed or else it atrophies. It requires creativity, curiosity, open-mindedness, risk-taking and perseverance ("Together for Learning: School Libraries and the Emergence of the Learning Comments," Ontario School Library Association, 2010).

TEACHER QUERIES

How can I "do inquiry" in a short amount of time?

Many teachers tell us, "I would like to try using an inquiry approach, but due to rotary timetabling restrictions, I have very little time to teach my subject." One suggestion is to arrange the class into groups and provide each group with a source from a different perspective. Have each group view their piece of evidence and discuss the perspective it presents. Then have each group share their findings with the whole class or do a jigsaw activity. Before exiting, have the students complete an exit card or journal reflecting on the inquiry question.

If you only see a class for one period per week, one suggestion is to chunk the inquiry. For example, in a health class the inquiry question may be, "How healthy is my lifestyle?" Each week, learners could focus on collecting data on a different aspect of their health (e.g., sleep, emotional/mental state, exercise/activity, diet, etc.) and organize that data in a table. The data could be compared to data from Statistics Canada (statcan.gc.ca) along with recommendations from health experts.

INQUIRY IN ACTION

Encouraging divergent thinking in your students

A grade 2 teacher asked her students how they might estimate the height of the classroom. Immediately, 20 hands shot up. One student replied, "We could put on suction cup boots and climb up the wall, and every giant step would be about one metre." A different student proposed, "The teacher could put a student on her shoulders and then add the height of the teacher plus the student." Another suggestion was, "We can make a tower with blocks and count up all the blocks."

A grade 7 teacher asked his class a similar question: "How could we estimate the surface area of the classroom, so we could know how much paint to buy to cover the room?" He heard crickets. So he prompted students to notice the shape of the wall and to recall the area rule for a rectangle. After some wait time and encouragement to think, students noticed the wall was built from concrete and they concluded that the concrete blocks could be counted. The number of blocks that made up the wall multiplied by the height of one block would give the approximate height of the room, and similarly with the length and width.

These two vignettes demonstrate how divergent thinking can atrophy when learners become accustomed to the teacher providing the right answers. Intermediate students may require some think time and encouragement to flex their thinking skills.

4.3 How can I help learners gather information, data and evidence?

In today's Internet age, we are faced with an avalanche of information. Our role as educators has shifted from being knowledge providers to facilitators in helping students process information and learn how to learn.

Our students come to us with varying degrees of competence in evaluating information. Some challenges include:

- not knowing what a credible source looks like,

- being overwhelmed by too much information, and

- material that is above their reading level.

In their report *Young Canadians in a Wired World Phase III* (2013), MediaSmarts confirms that the Internet is overwhelmingly the place students turn to when completing school work. In grade 4, 62% of Canadian students said they prefer using the Internet to complete school work and by grade 11, it was 91%. Adolescents reported using Google and Wikipedia most often, despite warnings from their teachers about Wikipedia's credibility. In his article "Can History be Open Source? Wikipedia and the Future of the Past," Rosenzweig (2006) concludes that "teachers have little more to fear from students' starting with Wikipedia than from their starting with most other basic reference sources. They have a lot to fear if students *stop* there." The solution is not to caution students against using Wikipedia, but to teach them about the limitations of reference resources, including its inherent bias. You may also suggest using a fact-checked reference resource, such as canadianencyclopedia.ca and at least three to five other sources.

Beyond reference materials, learners should engage in the objective viewing of primary sources, for example at a museum. Students may also use virtual galleries and virtual museums, such as Ontario Science Centre virtual tour, virtualmuseum.ca or historymuseum.ca to explore a range of primary sources.

BIG IDEA

Learners require differentiated levels of scaffolding and support when gathering sources.

FOOD FOR THOUGHT

"As we increasingly move toward an environment of instant and infinite information, it becomes less important for students to know, memorize or recall information, and more important for them to be able to find, sort, analyze, share, discuss, critique and create information. They need to move from being simply knowledgeable to being knowledge-able."

Michael Wesch

COMMITMENT
Does the need for gathering a range of diverse perspectives modify your commitment to doing inquiry?

CONTEXT
How would you assess your students' abilities to gather data and evidence?

CONVICTION
Relative to other goals in education, how critical is it for educators to help students analyze, synthesize and draw conclusions?

You may also wish to direct your learners to online databases. Your teacher-librarian can provide students with passwords for databases your school board subscribes to. There are also a number of free online databases, as well as databases through your public library. Some popular databases include:

- Ontario Education Resource Bank
- Pebble GO
- Global Issues in Context
- Canada Reference Centre
- Explora Canada
- TumbleBook
- Teen Health and Wellness

Evidence bundles

To save time or to direct learners to appropriate sources, you may wish to provide them with preselected resources or an evidence bundle. It should include sources that can be accessed by learners of all abilities. Sources from mainstream media, as well as alternative media, should be explored. Ideally, the evidence should present at least three perspectives: in favour of, disproving and neutral. In doing so, students must construct their own interpretation of the evidence.

Some websites contain their own evidence bundles. The Critical Thinking Consortium has "inquiry-pacs" that contain a variety of primary and secondary sources on a range of curriculum content topics (tc2.ca). The Multicultural History Society of Ontario has a bank of rich, ready-to-use student resources (www.mhso.ca/tiesthatbind/LearningResources.php). A number of sites also contain an inquiry question along with a resource to explore and investigate, such as smarterscience. youthscience.ca/inquiry-cards. These activities are labelled as structured, guided or open.

Helping students locate appropriate sources

1. Provide students with evidence bundles.

2. Direct learners to five sources (e.g., books or websites) that you have previewed and determined useful and credible.

3. Use bookmarking web technology (e.g., Diigo, Del.icio.us, Shelfari) for building reading lists.

4. Have learners work within walled garden websites (a browsing environment with restricted access to materials).

5. Explicitly teach and model how to narrow an Internet search.

6. Include the use of at least one human resource (e.g., librarian, museum curator, community member, parent) in your list of search criteria.

7. Steer learners away from simply typing their question into an internet search bar or using Q & A sites (e.g., WikiAnswers, Yahoo Answers) because the authority and credibility of the posters cannot be confirmed.

FIGURE 4.6 There are many ways to help students gather appropriate sources.

History evidence bundle

Here is an example of an evidence bundle used by a grade 8 history teacher.

Curriculum learning goal: To assess the differences in rights and privileges experienced by various groups in Canada from 1850–1914.

Inquiry question: Would you have wanted to be a Chinese Canadian between 1850 and 1914?

Source 1: Community leaders, elders or associations

Ask a community member to speak to your class about the Chinese rail labourers. Contact your local Chinese Benevolent Association or other Chinese-Canadian community groups with your specific question(s). Perhaps a community member would be willing to speak to your class. If distance is an issue, you could Skype or FaceTime.

Source 2: Head tax timeline

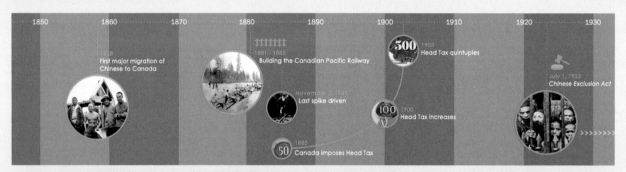

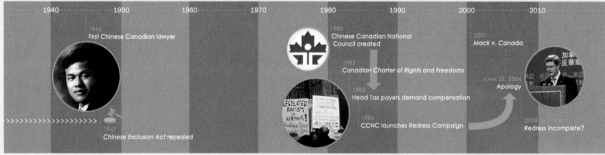

From roadtojustice.ca (courtesy of the Metro Toronto Chinese and Southeast Asian Legal Clinic).

Source 3: Stephen Harper's apology for Chinese head tax

Prime Minister Stephen Harper greets Chinese head tax survivor James Pon in Ottawa on June 22, 2006, during a ceremony announcing the government's official apology for the tax. (Tom Hanson/The Canadian Press)

Source 4: Photographs

Chinese railway workers' log camp beside railroad. From collectionscanada.gc.ca.

A Chinese work gang for the Great Northern Railway, circa 1909.

Source 5: Gordon Lightfoot's "Canadian Railway Trilogy"

Play the song "Canadian Railway Trilogy" by Gordon Lightfoot on YouTube and provide the lyrics.

Source 6: Heritage Minutes: Nitro

Play the Heritage Minute film "Nitro," which can be found at historicacanada.ca.

Source 7: Newspaper account of Chinese death

"Here in British Columbia along the line of the railway, the Chinese workmen are fast disappearing under the ground. No Medical attention is furnished nor apparently much interest felt for these poor creatures. We understand that Mr. Onderdonk declines interfering, while the Lee Chuck Co. (labour contractors), that brought the Chinamen from their native land, refused, through their agent Lee Soon, who is running the Chinese gang at Emory, to become responsible for doctors and medicine." *Yale Sentinel* (1883), quoted in Berton, Pierre. *The Last Spike*. Toronto: Anchor Canada, 1971.

Source 8: Telegraph transcript

The Great North Western Telegraph Co. To: Secretary of State in Ottawa, January 27, 1885:
"My ministers desire me to refer you to their Minute of

21st Nov [a letter or dispatch sent November 21st] … respecting destitution [poverty] among Chinese recently dismissed [laid off] from Dominion railway works [the C.P.R.], to request [that] I may be informed by telegraph how far [the] Dominion govt (government) will be prepared to assist in extending immediate relief [financial help] as considerable numbers of these wretched [miserable] creatures are now reduced to actual starvation."

[Signed] C.F. Cornwall
From a Source Doc created by The Critical Thinking Consortium, tc2.ca.

Source 9: Quote from John A. MacDonald

"At any moment when the Legislature of Canada chooses, it can shut down the gate and say, no more immigrants shall come here from China; and then no more immigrants will come, and those in the country at the time will rapidly disappear … and therefore there is no fear of a permanent degradation of the country by a mongrel race."

PM John A. Macdonald, House of Commons, April 30, 1883
From mhso.ca/tiesthatbind.

Source 10: *Spirits of the Railway* by Paul Yee

Read aloud the historical fiction short story "Spirits of the Railway" from *Tales from Gold Mountain* by Paul Yee.

Choosing a search engine

Most students are familiar with Google, but what about other search engines? Have them perform a search on Google, Bing, Ask, Yahoo Search, DuckDuckGo, KidzSearch, GoGooligans, Yahooligans, KidsClick!, Factmonster, SortFix, SweetSearch or others. Kiddle, Middlespot or other visual search engines can provide photographs, paintings and visual evidence. Vimeo, Bing Videos and many other video sites can offer alternatives to YouTube. Ask learners about the benefits or restrictions of different search engines. Have them reflect on which search engine they found the most useful and why.

Have your students type a query into the search bar of different search engines and notice how each site autocompletes or recommends related searches. For example, the name of politician Hillary Clinton is typed into Google, and the recommended searches are "age," "makeup" and "net worth." On Yahoo, the recommendations are "ill" and "hospitalized." Using Bing, the recommended searches are "Twitter," "news" and "crime accusations." We often make assumptions that the recommendations are based on the most popular searches; however, we must remember that search engines belong to corporations that may be filtering what we see with certain biases. Learners should be cautioned that the search results on different search engines can be biased and that they should search through different engines to get different results.

FIGURE 4.7 Do you know what search engines your students like best?

Modelled search and guided practice

Intermediate students may struggle when it comes to choosing effective search words or selecting the best results. Before engaging in Internet searches, we suggest that they view some short tutorials on how to use search tools, and then guide them through some practice with selecting effective search terms. Having students perform guided searches may help them remember and internalize it better than simply explaining how to do it.

Each search engine offers tutorials and videos that provide tips on how to parse a question or "pick the right search terms." Simply type *search engine name* + *search tutorial* or *how search works* into the search bar for a range of lessons.

Learners should be explicitly taught how to read a URL (or web address), including the domain name and domain extension. For example, .com is for a commercial site that is often trying to sell something, while .org is for organizations, usually providing information. Students can search for Canadian content by typing "site:.ca" in the search bar or "site:gc.ca" for a Canadian government site.

A common novice mistake when searching the Internet is typing the complete question into the search bar or using vague search terms. Guide students through parsing the question down to the keywords and then refining the search or narrowing it.

When overwhelmed with too many results, learners may become frustrated. It is important to model the inquiry disposition of perseverance and remind students that the first search may lead to a dead end and they will need to choose new search terms. Have them practice trying out different search word combinations, and let them know that you are available to help them refine their choice of words if they are experiencing difficulty. Assure them you are there to help them sift through the results of their search. Working in partners may also help as learners can bounce ideas off each other.

FOOD FOR THOUGHT

"Tell me and I'll forget. Show me and I may remember. Involve me and I'll understand."

Adage

TECH-ENABLED INQUIRY

Using Google

If you are using Google, the following videos are very helpful:

- https://www.youtube.com/watch?v=BNHR6IQJGZs
- https://www.youtube.com/watch?v=oFxkO2HlFRM

The latter video demonstrates how the search for "*endangered species*" gets 22 million hits, while the search *allintitle:"endangered species" site:gc.ca* provides just around 500 sites that are more applicable to the purpose of the inquiry.

Lesson plans for teachers are available at: https://sites.google.com/site/gwebsearcheducation/lessonplans

This slideshow provides pointers: https://docs.google.com/presentation/d/1JFaDwf3_mHVe-O0lqlGRibCD_Hv6zle58YsbUcanzDM/edit#slide=id.i0

Search tips

- Use a few simple terms.
- Nouns are better than adjectives or verbs.
- Use descriptive and specific words, not general words.
- Try synonyms or related words.
- Use words likely to appear in the title or text often.

FIGURE 4.8 Following a few basic tips can make a big difference in a student's search results.

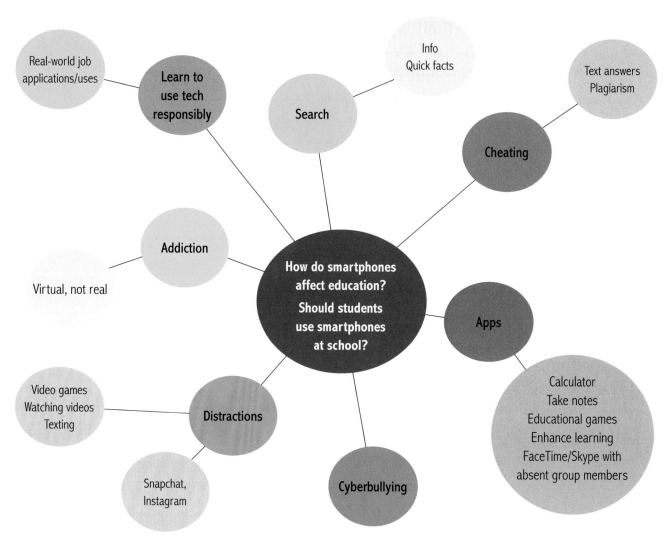

FIGURE 4.9 Brainstorming search terms for an inquiry about smartphone use in school will yield unique combinations of facts, issues, perspectives and concerns.

THINQ

- Who at your school has technological expertise and is good at Internet searches?

- How can the teacher-librarian, learning coaches or support personnel help?

Role of the intermediate teacher

In our work with teachers, a common question we hear is, "What is my role in helping students to *answer* the inquiry question?" Broadly speaking, teachers need to be both leaders — to guide and support students through the learning process — and co-learners, exploring new content and ideas alongside their students. However, we are sure that we frustrate teachers when we also say "it depends." In the same way that there is no "right" answer to an inquiry question, there is no one answer about a teacher's role. We say "it depends" because the role of the teacher during the actual inquiry is dependent on a number of considerations. These include: the abilities of the students in the class; the students' previous experience with research; whether or not students have access to technology in the classroom or library; how much time teachers have allotted to the inquiry in their planning; and the teacher's goals for this stage of the inquiry. Figure 4.10 may help you to determine the role you will play during the inquiry.

As you can see in Figure 4.10, if many of your students are not yet confident readers, do not have a great deal of research experience, and if Wi-Fi access in your classroom or library is unreliable, then this phase of the inquiry will probably need to be teacher-directed. It is worth noting that the role you play in one particular inquiry may not be the same as the role you will play in subsequent inquiries. As your students gain more experience with inquiry and develop specific inquiry skills, and as you gain more experience facilitating inquiry-based learning, your role will naturally evolve to meet the unique needs of your students from year to year.

CONVICTION
How does this role align with what you normally think of as your role?

More teacher direction	Determining your role during the investigative stage of an inquiry	Less teacher direction
Very little	Do my students have experience gathering and organizing evidence?	Quite a lot
Not yet	Are my students confident readers?	Pretty much
Not much	Do my students have experience doing research online?	Quite a lot
Not really	Do my students have convenient and reliable access to the Internet or library?	Yes absolutely
Very little	How much time do I have for this stage of the inquiry?	Quite a lot

FIGURE 4.10 Your role in an inquiry will depend upon the skills and experiences of your students and the conditions in your classroom.

The role of books

Intermediate students report that the Internet is easier to use than going to the library. You may wish to set criteria for the inquiry sources, such as using at least one book and one other non-website source. Intermediate learners may be unfamiliar with how to use text features (e.g., contents, index, headings, sidebars, bold, captions, etc.) to help them find specific information. A mini-lesson on using text features along with a class trip to the library can help encourage intermediates to use books. You may wish to discuss the pros (e.g., fact-checked, reliable) and cons (e.g., may be outdated) of books. If learners prefer using their tablets or laptops, suggest reading an e-book.

THINQ

- What are the advantages and disadvantages to providing students with evidence bundles?
- When would you release pieces of evidence one-by-one in a scaffolded manner, or all at once? What are the benefits or restrictions of each method?
- When would you prefer to provide your learners with evidence or have them seek out information independently? What are the advantages or disadvantages of each approach?
- When might it be more appropriate to select sources for students?
- Do your students embrace or dread research? Why might this be?
- How much time do you spend explicitly teaching Internet search skills?
- Where might you find local perspectives and non-mainstream perspectives?

STUDENT VOICE

"I like the inquiry project, but it took me forever to find information."

Harish, Grade 7 student

"I was trying to find information about murdered and missing Aboriginal women and girls, but most of the articles were too hard for me or I couldn't find the specific information I wanted."

Tamara, Grade 8 student

"I liked when my teacher got books for us on the topics we wanted to learn about because sometimes it's hard to find the right information on the Internet."

Kiesha, Grade 9 student

"We went on a class trip to the library, and my teacher helped us get a library card if we didn't have one. We got books and also magazines or videos to help with our research."

Tyrell, Grade 9 student

INQUIRY FOR ALL

Differentiating investigating and exploring

The investigating and exploring stage of inquiry should be differentiated, depending on the needs of the students. Learners may require varying degrees of support while gathering sources. You may wish to provide guided reading texts at various levels. For ESL and ELL students, you may paste a text into a Google Doc and use the translate feature to translate it into their first language. Text-to-speech apps or screen readers (e.g., Google TalkBack, Read&Write Gold) can provide reading support for some learners. Videos, vlogs, podcasts, audiobooks and photographs may also be accessible ways to gather information.

4.4 How do we determine if a source is accurate, reliable and credible?

Our intermediate learners may be skeptical of, or convinced by things they read on the Internet. Students should first consider the purpose of their search. If the inquiry is for science, dependable, objective, up-to-date data is required. If, on the other hand, the inquiry is for a writing class, then viewing opinion pages or debate sites may be appropriate to explore ideas. Remind students to read with a purpose in mind, by asking themselves, "Is this answering my question?"

Learners should check a website for the author's name and credentials. Check the about, background or biography section. Check if the author has been cited by others in Google Scholar. Consider who the publisher is. A website without a name is less reliable.

Reproducibles 4C, 4D, 4E and 4F offer different graphic organizers that may be used by students to assess the credibility of a source.

Organizers for evaluating sources	
PASS	purpose, accuracy, source, support
USEIT	usefulness, sources, evidence, impartial, thinking
SOURCE	source, objective, usefulness, reliability, context, evidence
FAN	for, against, neutral

FIGURE 4.11 Your students may find these tools helpful in thinking about how to evaluate sources.

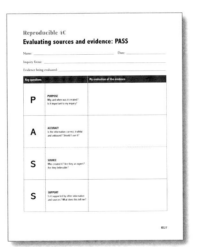

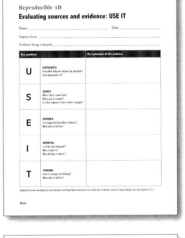

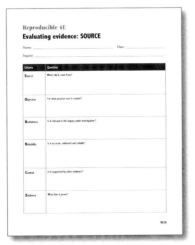

FIGURES 4.12–4.15 Reproducibles 4C, 4D, 4E and 4F, pp. RE27–RE30.

To help students develop a critical eye, we can provide a list of guiding questions, such as:

- Who created the website and why?
- What information about the type of website is contained in the web address (URL)?
- When was it published or updated? How current is the information?
- How reliable is the information? Can it be confirmed by other sources?
- How trusted is this website? Is it used by scholars?

CONTEXT
What are the greatest challenges you face in helping your students evaluate the usefulness and reliability of sources?

How will learners know when they have gathered enough evidence?

Students may want to know how many sources are required for an assignment. It is important for them to realize that it is the quality, not the quantity that matters. You may wish to provide guidelines or success criteria for sources:

1. At least two, preferably three or more perspectives/different points of view
2. Information from mainstream media (e.g., national broadcaster) and alternative media (e.g., small independent news agencies, credible bloggers)
3. At least one source in favour and one against
4. Age-appropriate and at an appropriate reading level (e.g., "I could understand the material")

A	Audience	Who is the intended audience (teens, kids, professors, conspiracy theorists, activists, conservatives, etc.)? Can you, as an audience, understand it?
P	Purpose	Who produced it and why (to inform, persuade, sell something, rant or complain)?
P	Process	Is the work cited with references? Has the work been checked by a publisher, peer reviewer, lawyers or editors?

FIGURE 4.16 The acronym APP can be posted on chart paper to remind students of the criteria for evaluating a source.

THINQ

- Are any of the graphic organizers new to you? Which will you try with your students?
- What criteria would you change or add to the "success criteria for sources"?

4.5 How can students organize their notes and keep track of their sources?

Once students have begun gathering resources and investigating materials, they need to take some notes and keep track of their sources. The method for storing notes and listing sources should be made clear from the beginning of the investigating and exploring stage. You may require a list of websites and book titles, or you may want fully sourced work in APA or MLA format. We should explicitly model for students how to take jot notes and track our sources.

Some ways to organize notes include:

- Use an electronic app, such as OneNote or Evernote to compile ideas.
- Keep a journal with two columns (one column with point form notes and the other column with source information).
- Type point form notes in a Google Doc. Click the Explore button in the lower right corner of the page and use the sidebar to find the source you want to cite. When you have found the appropriate source, click the three-dot button and choose which citation format you want to use (MLA, APA or Chicago)

CONTEXT

Does your school have a BYOD (bring your own device) policy to allow students to take notes on their phones or tablets?

CONFIRMATION

What successful strategies have you used to help learners record their thinking during this stage of the inquiry?

In Chapter 3, we introduced the KWHLAQ chart. During the questioning stage, learners are asked to complete K, W and H: what I know, what I want to know and how I will find out. During this second stage of the inquiry cycle, students should complete the L section of the chart, what they learned, and add to H, how they learned it. We provide two more graphic organizers, Reproducibles 4G and 4H, that can be used to help learners to organize their notes and clarify their thinking.

FIGURES 4.17–4.18
Reproducibles 4G and 4H, pp. RE31–RE32.

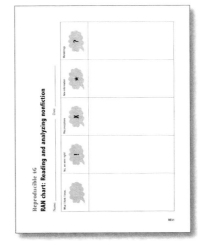

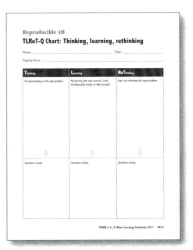

20 keywords strategy

Two issues can arise in the intermediate grades when students are answering open-ended questions:

- They may use their prior knowledge only and not seek out supporting or disproving evidence.
- They may copy and paste from the Internet.

To address these concerns, one helpful strategy is the 20 keywords strategy. Select a short text or article (1–2 pages). Complete a shared reading of the article and model how to select 20 or so keywords from the article. These words can be highlighted on a photocopied paper, electronically highlighted in a document or written down as notes on chart paper or in a journal. Remind students to cite the source. Next, repeat the activity as a guided activity, reminding learners to select only 20–25 words from the text to highlight or jot down. Finally have them summarize the content by only looking back at the selected keywords.

THINQ

- How will your students record and organize their thoughts, notes, observations and sources throughout the inquiry?
- How will you address students who "forget" their notes or "lose" them?

TEACHER QUERIES

How can I address plagiarism?

Despite being warned of the consequences, intermediate students will sometimes copy and paste from the Internet. Showing students that their work will be placed through a plagiarism checker and setting up criteria for sourcing work may help. If you suspect plagiarism, run it through a plagiarism checker and if it comes out as copied, have a one-on-one conversation with the student, offering a chance to redo the work. Another option is to ask the student to orally clarify the work. Sometimes telling students that what they said orally doesn't match what they submitted in writing lets them know the jig is up.

STUDENT VOICE

"I forgot to write down all the websites I was using for my research, and at the end I had to try and find them again for my references page, which was pretty impossible. Next time I'll try to remember to use the cite button as I go."

Hareesh, Grade 7 student

TEACHER VOICE

"An intermediate student handed in an assignment, and I noticed that it was missing a Works Cited or Reference page, so I asked the student where they got their information. The student replied that they 'used Google to get the information.' I realized that I had not explicitly taught my students what a website is, how to read a URL or how to cite a work. I shouldn't have assumed that these skills were already in place."

Intermediate teacher

4.6 How can I assess the investigating and exploring stage?

BIG IDEA

Formative assessment and feedback during the investigating stage of the inquiry can help learners move the inquiry forward.

It is important to carve out time during each stage of the inquiry to touch base with students and confirm that they are on a successful path. During the investigating and exploring stage of the inquiry, you may wish to use Reproducible 4I, *Assessing the investigating and exploring stage* or 4J, *Assessment planning template: Understands what is currently known*. To help students self-assess, we offer Reproducible 4K, *Inquiry rubric and self-check: Understands what is currently known* as a self-check. For your professional reflection, we have included Reproducible 4L, *Teacher checklist: Investigative mindset in my classroom*.

During a conference with a learner, you may wish to:

- Request a list of sources
- Ask how the learner's disposition or stance has changed as a result of the investigation
- Look at their point form notes/journals
- See how the student is feeling
- Have the learner self-assess their progress
- Reflect on how you can help them along

THINQ

- What criteria will you use to assess students during this stage of the inquiry?
- How will learners share their findings and wonderings so far with you and their peers?

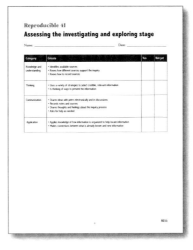

FIGURES 4.19–4.22 Reproducibles 4I, 4J, 4K and 4L, pp. RE33–RE36.

Revisit and reflect

In this chapter, we discussed the importance of gathering information from a wide range of perspectives, as well as ways to determine the purpose and credibility of a source. We explored the value of providing students with feedback about the information gathered before moving on to stage three. Suggestions for organizing notes and sources were provided.

THINQ

- How might your own confirmation biases influence the types of sources you introduce to your students?

- How might you improve the way you integrate multiple points of view in response to questions, issues or problems explored in your classroom?

- What strategies can you employ to improve your students' abilities to search for and locate answers to their inquiry question?

- What strategies can you employ to improve your students' abilities to assess the quality of sources and evidence they find?

BIG IDEAS

4.1 There are many ways to investigate and explore an inquiry question.

4.2 Learners should reflect on their assumptions or biases and collect evidence from a variety of perspectives.

4.3 Learners require differentiated levels of scaffolding and support when gathering sources.

4.4 Learners need to develop skills in assessing and evaluating the purpose and credibility of a source.

4.5 Learners benefit from watching others model how to organize notes and cite sources.

4.6 Formative assessment and feedback during the investigating stage of the inquiry can help learners move the inquiry forward.

Chapter 5
MAKING SENSE:
Creating new knowledge and innovative solutions

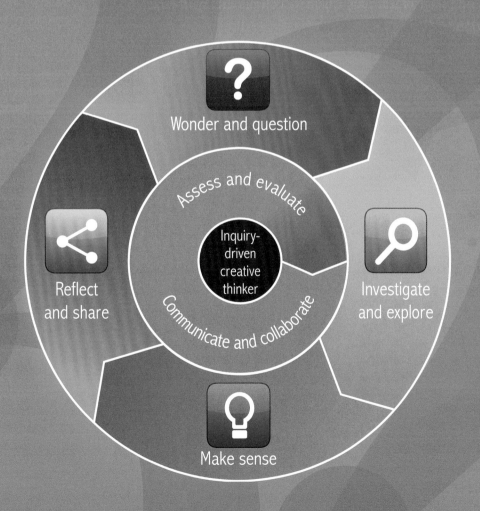

5.1 What does the "making sense" part of inquiry involve?

One of the most exciting parts of inquiry learning for intermediate students is when they arrive at the place where they can create new knowledge and innovative solutions. This is a generative stage of inquiry. Students have examined and explored what is already known; now they engage with this knowledge again in a new, creative, and highly personalized way.

You may recall that hopefulness is one of the four inquiry dispositions that we believe is essential to inquiry learning. Hopefulness is put into action when students can consider what is known and how things are in the world, and suggest innovations and alternative ways of thinking and being. In other words, when they create new knowledge. This is the empowering stage of learning, where we consolidate, synthesize and take action.

FIGURE 5.1 Unlike the *Investigate and explore* stage which is focused on "what is known," the *Make sense* stage gives students the opportunity to personally create new knowledge and understanding.

It is possible to shortchange student inquiry by placing too much emphasis on the investigation stage. Traditional research activities often honoured "what is known." Students were expected to memorize, summarize and perhaps retell in a creative way. Even when students created interesting final products to share, they were only retelling knowledge or posing solutions that already exist.

In this chapter, we pose some practical ideas on how to help intermediate students create new knowledge through the thinking skills of consolidation and synthesis. This will include suggestions on how to plan for a successful "making sense" stage of inquiry through intentional teaching and independent and group practice in the following areas:

- Model, scaffold and allow students to practice synthesizing and making sense of evidence.

- Use visual organizers specifically designed to help students make sense of their evidence.

- Directly teach "thinking boosts," "thinking traps" and practice thinking skills.

- Introduce empathy as an important skill and disposition in inquiry.

- Model, scaffold and allow students to practice the thinking skill of making a conclusion.

THINQ

- In your experience, in what ways do your students find it challenging to synthesize and/or consolidate evidence?

- What strategies do you use or think may help students in this stage of inquiry?

- How could you use the "Food for Thought" quotes to get your students thinking about the benefits of creating knowledge?

CONFIRMATION

Do your experiences with intermediate learners confirm that they can, if interested and engaged, generate creative and innovative solutions?

TEACHER QUERIES

How can I convince my students that "making" new knowledge through inquiry, and not just "learning" what is already known, is important to their lives?

Students already recognize that learning what is already known is an important part of being informed, skilled and "educated." They need to understand the difference between passive learning that depends on comprehension and memorization of cold hard facts, and active, deeper, personal and social learning. When faced with students who ask the teacher to "just tell me the answer" during inquiry learning, a teacher should return to the dispositions of inquiry learning to remind students that while it takes more time and effort, inquiry learning is ultimately of benefit to them.

You could remind students that an inquiry learner critically examines knowledge and generates their own knowledge, often through "real life" situations and problems that are of personal and social interest. Inquiry learning has the potential to change lives and the world as the learner interacts with knowledge. Passive learning leaves the world the same, since knowledge is not questioned for the purpose of change.

5.2 How can we help students consolidate their evidence?

Once students have finished the investigation phase of an inquiry and have gathered a variety of information, data or materials, they must make sense of it through consolidation. Consolidation means to bring together different ideas into a coherent whole. At this stage, students may ignore important information and have trouble making connections between different sources, but teachers can help students overcome these challenges in a number of ways.

Revisiting the inquiry question

As part of consolidation, ask students to return to their inquiry question. You can help them do this by distributing a consolidation template, such as Reproducible 5A, *Student exploration: Making sense of my inquiry*. Regardless of the tool you use to help your students make sense of their evidence, the following key questions should help them with the consolidation process.

Questions to focus consolidation

- What is my inquiry question? (What am I exploring?)
- What problem am I trying to solve?
- What did I think I might find?
- What did I find?
- What patterns or trends exist in the evidence?
- Can I make connections between pieces of evidence?
- Did I find anything surprising?
- What might have I overlooked?
- Am I able to draw a conclusion?
- Am I able to create something innovative?
- What questions remain?
- What additional questions do I now have?
- What could I do to explore this further?

FIGURE 5.3 Pausing between evaluating evidence and drawing a conclusion can be an important step that avoids difficulties later on.

BIG IDEA

Consolidation is a complex thinking process that requires teacher modelling and support.

FOOD FOR THOUGHT

"People do not like to think. If one thinks, one must reach a conclusion. Conclusions are not always pleasant."

Helen Keller

"It is a sign of intellectual maturity to always crawl to conclusions."

Mokokoma Mokhonoana

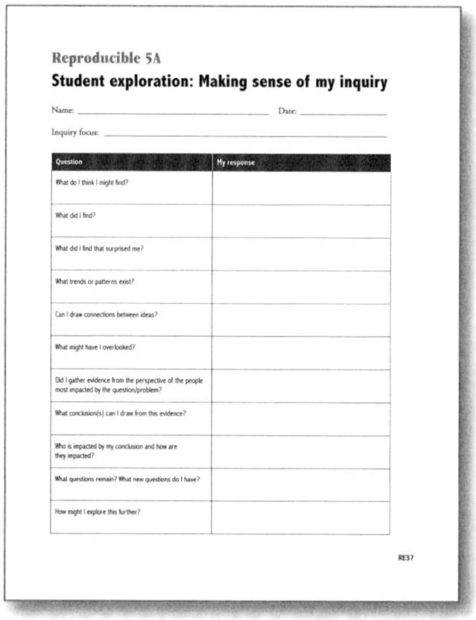
Reproducible 5A

Student exploration: Making sense of my inquiry

Name: ______ Date: ______

Inquiry focus: ______

Question	My response
What do I think I might find?	
What did I find?	
What did I find that surprised me?	
What trends or patterns exist?	
Can I draw connections between ideas?	
What might have I overlooked?	
Did I gather evidence from the perspective of the people most impacted by the question/problem?	
What conclusion(s) can I draw from this evidence?	
Who is impacted by my conclusion and how are they impacted?	
What questions remain? What new questions do I have?	
How might I explore this further?	

RE37

FIGURE 5.2 Reproducible 5A, p. RE37.

Identifying trends, patterns and connecting ideas

One way for students to consolidate their evidence is to identify patterns or trends in the information they have collected. Patterns or trends are ideas, themes or arguments that repeat throughout the evidence. Students can be prompted to identify patterns and trends by considering questions such as the ones in Figure 5.4.

When making sense of evidence, students can also look for connections between ideas. These connections can be between their *own* ideas and the evidence, or connections between the ideas *expressed in the evidence* they have collected. For example, students make connections between their own ideas and the evidence when they respond to the questions "What did I wonder?" and "What did I find?" Students will also make connections when they find three similar ideas expressed in the evidence they have collected.

What is **similar** about the evidence?

Are there **consistent characteristics** across a number of pieces of evidence?

Can you see any **patterns**? What do they tell you?

Can you see any **trends**? What do they tell you?

INQUIRY FOR ALL

Improving the usefulness of concept maps

Concept maps can help your students make connections between ideas and information. They can help students consolidate and make sense of evidence. Some teachers have their students create concept maps as a way to evaluate their thinking skills and knowledge of a topic, rather than giving a more traditional unit test.

Concept maps are not a new tool. Students know that they should: (1) start at the centre of the page and work outwards; (2) print clearly so the map is easy to read and understand; and (3) limit the information on the map to key words, images and visual aids like arrows or icons. Concept maps can be made more useful in the consolidation process with a few tweaks:

- Place keywords on connecting lines in the mind map to reinforce connections between ideas.
- Use colour to identify patterns and themes.
- Use three-dimensional elements to reinforce patterns and trends.
- If students run out of space, paste more paper onto the map. This will help make patterns and trends obvious.
- Choose colours, symbols or images to represent an idea or theme and use them directly on the concept map to draw connections between ideas and themes.
- Encourage students to use mind-mapping apps if they prefer them to pen and paper.

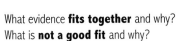

What evidence **fits together** and why? What is **not a good fit** and why?

FIGURE 5.4 Asking a few key questions can be very helpful when trying to make sense of a body of information, data and evidence.

Obstacles to effective synthesis

Synthesis can be a complicated intellectual process. It may be useful to discuss with your students the nature of the human brain, how it processes information and the potential errors it can make. Understanding these potential traps may help learners proceed more carefully when synthesizing and drawing conclusions. The table in Figure 5.5 discusses some of these thinking phenomena.

Type of error	Description	Implication for making sense
Treating inferences as facts	One way the human brain makes errors is by making inferences and then treating inferences as facts.	Without a fairly rigorous check and analysis to confirm the difference between what is factually true and what may be true, humans may rely on faulty information when making sense of new information.
Confirmation bias	The human brain has a tendency to search for or interpret information in a way that confirms what a person already believes.	When trying to make sense of new information or a body of evidence, humans tend to actively seek out and assign more weight to evidence that confirms their hypothesis and beliefs and ignore evidence that may refute them.
Memory bias	A memory bias either enhances or impairs the recall of a memory or alters the content of a reported memory.	For intermediate learners this means: • You are more likely to remember what you did or said yourself than what someone else tells you (**self-generation bias**). • The more times something is told to you, the more likely you are to believe it, whether it is true or not (**illusion of truth effect**). • Discussing a memory may affect your ability to remember it accurately (**misinformation effect**). • You may remember that two events are related when they are not (**illusory correlation**).

FIGURE 5.5 Do you think your students would be interested in learning about the different ways their brains might fool them?

THINQ

- Which of these brain errors do you recognize in yourself and your students?
- How could you run an activity about these brain errors with your students before beginning the synthesis process?

CONVICTION
Do you think you have any pet theories about teaching and learning that bias you against new approaches and possibilities?

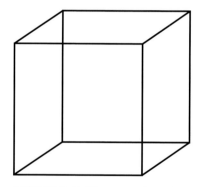

FIGURE 5.6 When you stare at this Necker Cube, the faces of the cube move forward and back. This "brain error" is a result of the fact that this is an ambiguous line drawing with no depth clues.

5.3 What are some simple tools to help students draw conclusions?

At the most basic level, drawing a conclusion is really about weighing the evidence related to a question or problem under investigation. Most inquiries will have a number of "branches" of exploration and associated evidence. After students have consolidated their evidence, they will have to make a decision about the inquiry question under investigation.

Keeping our intermediate learners in mind, we believe that it is important to provide tools that are clear and uncomplicated. Graphic organizers are a very helpful, especially to help student thinking in the inquiry process. Venn diagrams are useful to compare and contrast, and to consolidate evidence. Many teachers use a fishbone graphic organizer to help students draw conclusions (see Figure 5.7). The lines or bones at the top of the fish are where students record "what I know" in alignment with the bones at the bottom of the fish, where students record "what the evidence is telling me." The head of the fish is the conclusion that arises after consideration of the all the fishbones.

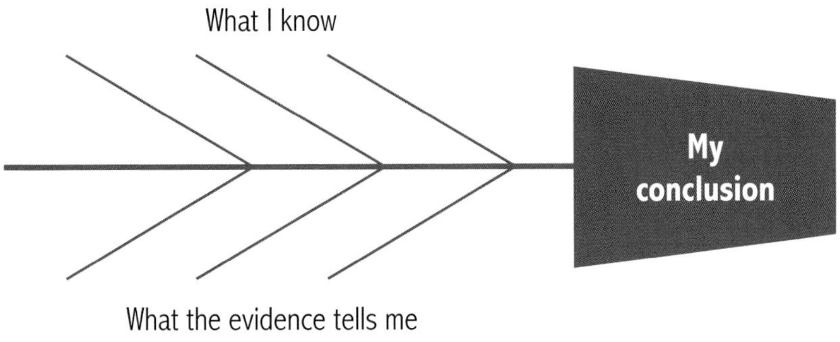

FIGURE 5.7 You can use a fishbone graphic organizer to help students draw conclusions.

BIG IDEA
Sound conclusions can be drawn only after a body of evidence is carefully weighed.

FOOD FOR THOUGHT

"We have the duty of formulating, of summarizing, and of communicating our conclusions, in intelligible form, in recognition of the right of other free minds to utilize them in making their own decisions."

Ronald Fisher

CONFIRMATION
What are your favourite tools to help students organize their thinking?

Many teachers also use PMI charts help them with the inquiry process. The PMI (Plus, Minus, Interesting) chart was developed by Edward de Bono in 1982. De Bono was an early proponent of the deliberate teaching of thinking in schools. The PMI chart has many applications, but it was designed to be a quick tool (three to five minutes in length) to weigh the pros and cons of an issue, widen the perception of a problem or decision, or uncover issues that might have been overlooked.

In the context of inquiry we have found that many teachers use PMI charts (without a 5-minute length limit) to help students draw conclusions. A blank template is provided as Reproducible 5B, but a simple web search will provide you with a number of other formats to choose from.

Another organizer to use to help students who have experience in drawing conclusions is the "What? So What? Now What?" chart. In the "What?" category students summarize their evidence. In the "So What?" category they identify the relevance of the evidence and draw conclusions. In the "Now What?" category student consider possible actions and innovations.

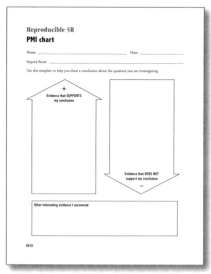

FIGURE 5.8 Reproducible 5B, p. RE38.

What?	So what?	Now what?
Summarize the evidence: • What happened? • What is known and not known? • What is agreed or not agreed on? • What did you expect and what was different?	Assess why the evidence is relevant: • What can be learned? • What was the impact on people and events? • Why does it matter? • What are the consequences and outcomes? • Who cares and why?	Consider possible actions and innovations: • What else do you need to find out? • What can you do with what you have learned? • What are the possibilities and opportunities? • What conclusions can you make, if any? • What can you do now that you couldn't before?

FIGURE 5.9 How and when might you use this organizer to help your students evaluate evidence and draw conclusions?

Weighing the evidence and concluding

Not all of the evidence students consider will be equally important or useful. Students need to weigh the evidence if they are to sort and filter their data. Figure 5.10 offers some criteria to consider. Reproducible 5C, *Balance of evidence* asks students to "pile up" the evidence they have in support of the inquiry question under investigation. The side with more evidence is the side they would argue answers the inquiry question. Although we do not want students to see inquiry questions as either "right" or "wrong," for the intermediate learner it is likely best not to complicate the process of drawing a conclusion with too many layers, at least in the beginning. Our hope is that as intermediate learners gain sophistication with the consolidation process, they will start to consider evidence that is ambiguous and illustrates the grey areas of their inquiry question.

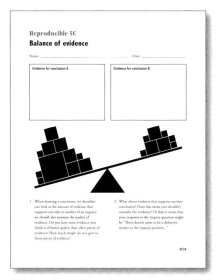

FIGURE 5.11 Reproducible 5C, p. RE39.

Is some evidence more important or useful in answering the inquiry question than other evidence?

Is there more evidence supporting one conclusion over others?

Does any of the evidence conflict?

FIGURE 5.10 Because not all of the evidence will be equally important or useful, it is important for intermediate learners to begin to weigh the value of the information relative to their objective.

5.4 How can we help students synthesize?

Synthesis is another complex thinking skill. It involves taking knowledge from multiple sources and combining them with our own knowledge and experiences to create new, fresh ideas. Students sometimes confuse synthesis with summary or consolidation. Summarizing is retelling. Consolidation is combining different evidence into a coherent picture. Synthesis is the combination of ideas to form a new idea, theory or innovation. Synthesis involves creativity whereas consolidation does not. Here are three activities that you could use to clarify and deepen student understanding of synthesis.

CONTEXT
How much synthesizing do your intermediate students do? What do they find most challenging about it?

Everyday synthesis

The GCFLearnFree.org video, "What Is Synthesis?" does a good job of clearly explaining how we synthesize in everyday life. It uses the example of a person trying to decide whether or not to see a new movie. The person asks a friend for their opinion, they check social media for some reviews, and they recall from their own experiences that they enjoyed previous movies in this genre and/or with the same actors. All of this information is combined in our thinking. We consider, reflect and synthesize the information to come up with our own decision; in this case, the person decides to wait until the movie is available on Internet streaming since they are not really interested in the movie, and it doesn't top the list of ones they want to spend time and extra money going to the theatre to see.

This example of "everyday synthesis" is extended in inquiry learning when we ask students to answer their inquiry questions by critically considering several perspectives and then creatively combining those perspectives with their own individual values, thinking and perspectives for the goal of creating new knowledge. You could show this video to your students or describe the scenario to them and ask them to think of a time in recent memory where they used the skill of synthesis. Student stories should be shared with the class. The idea that synthesis is a frequently-used skill of thinking should help students take risks when they are called on to synthesize evidence from an inquiry.

Using visual metaphors

Getting students to examine visual metaphors that illustrate the meaning of synthesis can help them to deepen their understanding of the word. There are many visuals available on the Internet. Students could discuss what these visuals represent and which ones they feel best represent the act of synthesis or creating new knowledge. They could be encouraged to create their own visual in yet another act of synthesis!

Using the metaphor of "mashup" as creative synthesis

Intermediate students are familiar with the term "mashup" from social media and popular culture. A mashup occurs when a musical, visual or multimedia artist takes two or more very different products and makes them into a unique new product. For example, when a musician takes the vocal soundtrack from a song from the 1970s and seamlessly merges it in a creative way into the instrumental track of a current hip hop song. In the world of web applications, "mashups" occur when date and/or functionality from different sources are combined (e.g., combining Google Maps with Wikipedia).

Students can begin to see themselves as creative "mashup artists." They take ideas, solutions or products that already exist and combine them with other ideas, solutions, perspectives and/or products, and create something that is completely new. Students may relate to the idea that the mashup is ultimately "better" than the originals due to the creative innovation that results in a new product. Get students to identify mashups in music, art and online. Ask them to discuss the purpose of mashups and what the criteria of a good mashup might be. This criteria will be similar to criteria for effective synthesis.

FIGURE 5.12 This is one example of a visual metaphor for synthesis, but there are many more.

Innovation as creative synthesis

The idea of mashup can be extended to the realm of product innovation, where a product is created as the result of imagination and synthesis. The product created should be of value to its intended audience. Students can view popular television shows where innovators pitch their business ideas. They could be asked to deconstruct the innovative product by asking, "What is the problem they are trying to solve?" "How has the innovator used synthesis by combining old and new ideas?" and "Does the innovation have 'value' to you, to society, to a business?" Students can also examine scientific innovations with the same questions in mind. Inquiry learning in the STEM disciplines typically involves the skill of product innovation.

Practising synthesis

Once students have a good grasp on what synthesis is, they are ready to practice it on their own and with others. Knowledge-building circles are one way to promote collaborative and independent synthesis. Reproducible 5D, *Practicing synthesis* outlines a "bite-size" synthesis activity to be used as practice and to provide potential formative assessment for you and your students.

Knowledge-building circles

Knowledge-building circles are powerful places to create new knowledge collaboratively. While collaborative groups in a circle formation have been the habit in many student-centred classrooms, we came across the idea of an inquiry-focused knowledge-building circle in Lorraine Chiarotto's book *Natural Curiosity* (2011). While that text focuses on outdoor environmental experiences and inquiries for early childhood, the idea adapts well to intermediate learners. It also supports the idea of collaborative and independent synthesis.

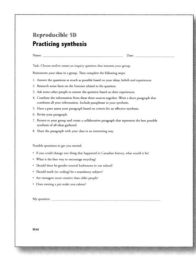

FIGURE 5.13
Reproducible 5D, p. RE40.

The next time the knowledge-building circle meets, students talk about possible sources to examine and potential experts to have conversations with. This could include Internet sources, academic writing, community experts, parents, educators and other students whose interests are at stake when solving the problem and/or answering the question. At the end of this knowledge-building circle, students agree to what sources they will examine. Groups of students may choose or be assigned to different sources.

After taking time to critically investigate the sources, students come back to the knowledge-building circle to discuss their findings, assess the sources and determine if other sources are needed. At this point in the process, knowledge-building circles can be subdivided into smaller collaborative groups where students are tasked to use innovative and creative synthesis to come up with an answer to the questions and/or problem. A final whole-class knowledge-building circle can occur once smaller groups have had a chance to create their own knowledge.

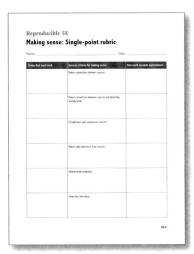

FIGURE 5.14 Reproducible 5E, p. RE41.

Assessing students as they make sense

Students should co-construct what they think are the important criteria of synthesis after engaging in practice synthesis activities. They should be encouraged to self- and peer-assess their synthesis activities based on one or two of these criteria at a time. Teachers should observe and conference with students in order to ascertain next steps in teaching and to provide feedback in real-time. Reproducible 5E, *Making sense: Single point rubric* lays out some possible assessment criteria for your consideration.

THINQ

- How do you already use the strategy of a knowledge-building circle? In what ways could you adapt and modify its use in inquiry learning with your students?

- Considering the potential criteria for synthesis, where do you think your students need the most direct teaching and practice?

- How do you encourage student ideas and experiences as an important part of synthesis?

5.5 How can we help students make sense with empathy?

Over our years of work in intermediate classrooms, we have noted that the most meaningful inquiry learning experiences ask students to develop and use empathy. If empathy is not an explicit part of inquiry learning, then our new knowledge and innovative products lack "heart."

Why empathy matters

Empathy asks that we consider the feelings, beliefs and needs of others while we inquire. This is challenging but important work as the *Food for Thought* quote by Martin Hoffman suggests. Empathy is ideally both a shared feeling *and* an accurate understanding of another person's experiences and beliefs. Empathy is not necessarily agreement, but it is an honest attempt to "walk in the shoes" of others.

Roman Krznaric is a philosopher noted for his work on empathy. In his book *Empathy: Why it matters and how to get it* (2010), he elaborates on the six habits of highly empathic people. Two of these traits are the same as the attributes we identify as important for an inquiry learner, namely, being curious about people and developing what he calls an "ambitious imagination." The other habits are "challenging prejudices and discover commonalities," "trying another person's life," "listening hard and opening up" and "inspiring mass action and social change." Students may benefit from viewing the Royal Society of Arts' animated video, "The Power of Outrospection," based on Krznaric's argument that empathetic people are not only nicer to others, they are more innovative in their thinking and tend to create more valuable and meaningful things and ideas to benefit society. They are also more likely to help others in need.

Inviting empathy throughout the inquiry

Invite your students to think about who is most affected by certain inquiry questions and who is most impacted by certain inquiry conclusions. They should be aware that inquiry learning involves the skills of considering multiple perspectives and examining biases and assumptions, both our own and those of other people.

WORDS MATTER

Empathy
The ability to understand and share the feelings of another.

FOOD FOR THOUGHT

"This is a wonderful planet, and it is being completely destroyed by people who have too much money and power and no empathy. "
Alice Walker

"Since there's no viable alternative, empathy may be the only glue available to help conflicting groups achieve the social cohesion, conflict resolution, and cooperation needed to save the planet. So, empathy must be kept alive."
Martin L. Hoffman

"Empathy involves appreciating how others make their judgments. Self-knowledge requires knowing how I make my judgments. Speaking practically, self-knowledge and empathy are two sides of the same coin."
Wynn Schwartz

Empathetic students understand that everyone has their own point of view and they know that their own perspective is not universal. Empathetic students can identify feelings in themselves and others and they know that thoughts and feelings have a strong influence on what we feel and what we do.

When gathering sources, intermediate students should connect with other people who have direct experience with the topic in question and approach them with genuine curiosity. They may connect with a family member, other students and community members. Discuss with students the fact that judging other people is something we all do. It is not a good or bad thing in itself. Students can be made more aware of how previous judgments of others have impacted their lives and their thinking. We can talk about how we can use attentive listening and genuine curiosity to withhold judgment in order to first gain understanding.

When students are asked to synthesize ideas, they can feel most confident in their new knowledge or innovative solution if they have thought deeply about what others feel, think and believe. Incorporating drama, non-fiction texts and documentary analysis into your inquiry learning may result in greater student empathy and a more empathetic inquiry result.

THINQ

- Why do you think empathy sometimes "falls away" in problem solving?

- How do you help your students "walk in the shoes" of others?

- What and who could support you in infusing more empathy in inquiry learning?

INQUIRY IN ACTION

Remembering empathy during inquiry

Jennifer's class was curious and motivated to solve a problem. They had researched the conditions of many First Nations communities. The focus of the inquiry turned to the lack of access to drinkable water. The inquiry question became "How can we create a water purification system to help the people in this community?"

Jennifer's class dove into scientific and engineering data on how to create water purification systems. The class designed what they thought could be a portable and cost-effective water purification system. At the end of the inquiry the students celebrated their success in solving the problem. Jennifer realized that something was missing. While the inquiry had begun in a place of curiosity and care, it quickly moved into an information gathering activity that did not include the perspectives or experiences of First Nations people. The problem had not been solved and the issue had not been examined in a truly empathic way.

Jennifer shared her concerns with her grade partner. Their conversations resulted in Jennifer's decision to return to the inquiry experience once again with an empathetic focus. She reviewed the water purification models and asked her students the following questions: "Why might First Nations people reject our inventions?" "What problem have we solved with our inventions?" "What problem have we not solved?" "If we were to ask a First Nations person what their life was like and what problems they face, what do you think they would say?" "What does it feel like to not have access to drinking water?" "What does it feel like to be a community that does not have safe drinking water when the majority of communities do?"

She reflected on ways to ensure empathy was part of future inquiry activities. She thought about integrating drama strategies, nonfiction literature and documentaries based on the lives of people living in these communities and how she might connect with First Nations people to infuse inquiry with empathy.

5.6 How can students avoid "thinking traps" and instead use "thinking boosts"?

The making sense stage of inquiry is an elaborate dance involving many critical thinking and creative steps. This generative stage can be particularly challenging for all learners, not just intermediate students. When looking at student work during this stage, we have found some common "thinking traps" in the work of intermediate learners. Some of these common traps include "black-and-white" thinking, egocentric thinking and lazy thinking. Students may plagiarize, fall prey to irrelevant information, meander in their thinking or set out to prove that their original idea was correct despite conflicting evidence.

As you read over Figure 5.17, *Thinking traps and thinking boosts*, consider your students and your teaching experience. Which traps do your students fall into? Which traps seem prevalent in society, and not just in our intermediate students? What could you do to get your students to recognize and avoid these thinking traps and to focus instead on practising thinking boosts?

How do I assess the consolidation phase of the inquiry process?

In Chapter 2, *Assessment and evaluation*, we suggested that the six essential abilities of inquiry learners are the core of inquiry activities and inquiry assessment. The abilities to make sense, synthesize and consolidate are crucial at every stage of an inquiry. For example, a student cannot formulate a response to an inquiry question without "asking questions" about the evidence they have collected and they cannot conclude an inquiry without consolidation or "putting it all together." Reproducible 5F, *Assessment planning template: Puts it all together* can be used to plan your triangulated assessment evidence collection. Reproducible 5G, *Inquiry rubric and self-check: Puts it all together* can be used as an assessment for and as learning tool.

FIGURES 5.15–5.16
Reproducibles 5F and 5G, pp. RE42–RE43.

Thinking traps	Thinking boosts
Lazy thinking Thinking is hard and you will avoid it if possible. You tend to accept other people's thinking and don't question it as you should.	**Active thinking** You strive for your best thinking and practice your thinking; you ask deep questions, listen and read carefully, analyze what is being said and ask questions
Thinking reproductively Your thinking is based on other people's thinking without asking "Is this reasonable?" or "Is this right?"	**Thinking productively** Your thinking is based on your desire to problem solve reasonably and ethically.
Drifting and aimless thinking When thinking meanders and is off-topic; when it incorporates a lot of "extra" words and information that is not relevant.	**Sticking to the point** When thinking is relevant, logical and makes important connections.
Being unreasonable Errors in reasoning (i.e., fallacies) happen when you make inferences or draw conclusions that are faulty, illogical or unsubstantiated.	**Being reasonable** Reason demands that you can recognize a sound argument and valid evidence and that you can create your own sound arguments based on valid evidence.
Black-and-white thinking Thinking that relies exclusively on labels like good or bad, right or wrong, weak or strong.	**Shades of grey** Thinking that considers and searches for many nuances and perspectives.
Groupthink Your thinking mirrors your friends (or your nation's, or your religion's thinking).	**Analytical thinking** Analyzing group influences in your thinking. Asking yourself, "Why do I believe this to be true?"
It's all about me! Egocentric thinking prevents us from expanding our thinking and makes us think we are the centre of the universe and never wrong.	**Open-mindedness and realism** Consider and accept the fact that you are wrong or ill-informed some of the time. Be open-minded, empathetic and try to accept constructive feedback on your thinking.
Setting out to prove you were right You tend to accept information and ideas that confirm what you already think, believe, know and do, and dismiss evidence to the contrary.	**Setting out to see multiple perspectives** Gain awareness of your own biases and assumptions. Seek to find other perspectives to challenge or expand your thinking.
You know what I mean? Assuming that there is a common understanding of the big ideas in your topic or argument such as "justice," "freedom," "democracy," "rights," "fair," "sustainability."	**Define your terms!** Define your terms so others may understand your perspective.
Negative thinking Negative thinking leads to frustration in life and in learning.	**Positive thinking** Positive thinking provides fuel to keep your thinking going.
What do you mean? Communicating without clarity.	**I get your point!** Communicate one point at a time. Elaborate on your meaning clearly. Give appropriate examples. Avoid using too many words and phrases in a sentence.
Plagiarizing Taking someone else's ideas and passing them off as your own.	**Summarizing** Learn how to summarize and how to correctly cite sources. If you don't know how, here is a short tutorial to teach you: *You Quote It, You Note It!* A 10 minute animated tutorial that would be appropriate for intermediate students. http://library.acadiau.ca/sites/default/files/library/tutorials/plagiarism/

FIGURE 5.17 Which of these types of thinking are common among your intermediate students?

Revisit and reflect

This chapter looked at how teachers can best help students "make sense" of the evidence they collect or are given during an inquiry. We shared our belief that it is worth taking the time to help students understand that hard thinking is involved at this stage of inquiry and all people are prone to thinking traps when selecting and analyzing information. We also shared our belief that empathy is an important component of making sense if student knowledge creation and innovative solutions are to have meaningful impact on them and on others.

We explored a number of ways that teachers can assist students with the making sense process, including:

- Having students revisit inquiry questions;

- Working deliberately with concept maps and visual organizers;

- Identifying patterns and trends in evidence and making connections between ideas;

- Providing tools to help students draw conclusions;

- Having students deepen their understanding of synthesis by practicing synthesis; and

- Encouraging students to "walk in the shoes" of others as they generate new knowledge and innovative solutions.

To conclude your exploration of this chapter, take some time to complete Reproducible 5H: *Teacher checklist: Synthesis and consolidation in my classroom.*

THINQ

- Which of the big ideas in this chapter do you feel are the most important and enduring understandings for you?

- How might you collaborate with your colleagues to increase your confidence and expertise at facilitating this step of the inquiry process?

- What do you think your next step will be in regards to helping your students improve their capacity to make sense of what they find through inquiry?

BIG IDEAS

5.1 The final stages of inquiry learning involve consolidation and synthesis in order to create new knowledge and innovative solutions.

5.2 Consolidation is a complex thinking process that requires teacher modelling and support.

5.3 Sound conclusions can be drawn only after a body of evidence is carefully weighed.

5.4 We can help students synthesize to create new knowledge.

5.5 The making sense stage of the inquiry should involve empathy.

5.6 Students can learn to avoid thinking traps and use thinking boosts when making sense and creating new knowledge.

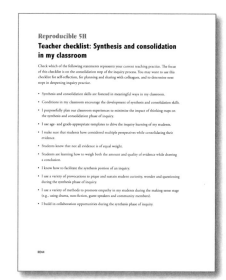

FIGURE 5.18 Reproducible 5H, p. RE44.

Chapter 6

REFLECTION AND SHARING:
Pushing inquiry learning to a deeper level

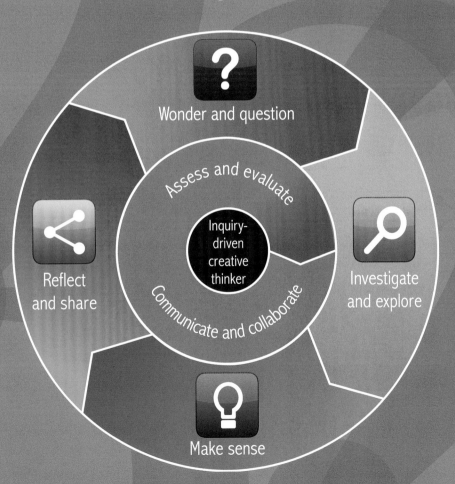

6.1 Why does reflection and sharing matter?

You'll notice that in our inquiry process cycle (Figure 6.1), we have reflection and sharing as a final, explicit component. The goal of this endpoint reflection and sharing is to push student thinking to a deeper level. Sharing and reflection activities are an essential element of *all stages* of an inquiry; for example, during the questioning, investigating, or making sense "stages" of the inquiry process. However, at an end point of an inquiry, students should be given time to consolidate and articulate key lessons learned.

Without this opportunity to synthesize and consolidate through reflection and sharing, students may be left with the impression that inquiry is a series of isolated steps or disconnected activities that end in the creation of some kind of product. On their own, they may not be able to move from surface knowledge and skills to the significant changes in cognitive structures that define deep learning.

BIG IDEA

Inquiry learning becomes deep learning through reflection and sharing.

CONVICTION

How convinced are you that reflection and sharing can deepen learning?

FOOD FOR THOUGHT

"We don't learn from experience, we learn by reflecting on experience."
John Dewey

"Great minds discuss ideas. Average minds discuss events. Small minds discuss people."
Eleanor Roosevelt

"Education is not the learning of facts but the training of the mind to think."
Albert Einstein

"By three methods we may learn wisdom: First, by reflection, which is noblest; second, by imitation, which is easiest; and third by experience, which is the bitterest."
Confucius

"When you learn, teach. When you get, give."
Maya Angelou

"Everyone you ever meet will know something that you don't."
Bill Nye

FIGURE 6.1 Even though reflection and sharing occurs throughout the inquiry process, setting it out as a final step in the process is intended to emphasize the need for and critical importance of helping students consolidate what they have learned through inquiry.

Good reflection promotes metacognition, or thinking about one's thinking. Reflection helps students to achieve a clearer understanding of what they have done through inquiry and who they are as learners. It allows the learner to revisit and reinterpret understandings and strategies through introspection and dialogue.

In each chapter of this book we have highlighted opportunities where students can reflect and share. In this chapter we want to push learning deeper by encouraging teachers to plan for rich reflection and sharing at the endpoint of an inquiry cycle.

CAPACITY

What are the big obstacles you encounter in incorporating more reflection and sharing at the end point of an inquiry process?

INQUIRY IN ACTION

Does reflection promote metacognition?

Not all cognitive processing requires metacognition and not all learners engage in metacognition. It is possible to engage in mental operations that involve memory, attention, language, reasoning and problem solving and to not think about them. However, metacognitive skills can be taught. Metacognition is a type of cognition that can deepen thinking and improve learner motivation and self-efficacy.

Emma's grade 8 students are practising identifying the main points in a two-page reading. The students need cognitive skills to read, comprehend and identify the main points in the reading. They will also need to use their metacognition to think about the processes they will use to identify the main points. This metacognitive thinking might involve strategies such as "I'm going to use a highlighter or post-it notes to identify the main points," "I'm going to skim and scan the passage first to help me identify the potential main points, then I will read more carefully since I usually miss something the first time through," or "I'm going to look for words and ideas that are repeated in the text since that's a clue to what's important." In these examples of self-talk, the students are thinking about their own cognitive processes. These metacognitive processes are intentionally and purposefully allocating mental resources to cognitive tasks. Reflections that focus on metacognition are an effective way to get students to think metacognitively, increasing their independence and motivation as learners.

INQUIRY IN ACTION

Thinking about reflection and sharing

Post a selection of "Food for thought" quotes in your classroom. Provide chart paper for students to write on next to each quote. Have students move from one quote to another in small groups and write their thoughts, questions and connections in response to the quote and other students' comments. Debrief new learning with the whole class based on the inquiry questions "Why should I/we reflect on my/our learning?" and "Why should I/we share my/our learning?"

6.2 What does effective reflection and sharing look and sound like?

BIG IDEA

Students and teachers need concrete examples of what good reflection and sharing look and sound like.

To paraphrase John Dewey, we do not learn from inquiry experiences — we learn from reflecting on inquiry experiences. Reflection asks us to pause and pay attention to our thinking and to make changes to our thinking. In our everyday lives, we typically reflect only when something goes wrong or when something surprises us. These are the moments when we revisit our experiences to try and figure out the unusual or surprising event. In education, however, we reflect as professionals and we ask our students to reflect (whether they are inclined to or not) to grow their capacity to think deeply.

Effective reflection

Reflection begins with contemplation and introspection. A student needs to get into his or her own mind and ponder deeply, assisted by a prompt or protocol provided by the teacher. It is important to allow students this time of silence to hear their thoughts and connect with their feelings.

The next stage of reflection involves dialogue with others. Through our conversations, our reflections can become more action-oriented. Sharing reflections allows students to hear diverse views on how other people make sense, how they were feeling, and what strategies and actions support their learning.

CONFIRMATION

How has sharing and reflecting with colleagues helped clarify your thinking and improved your professional practice?

STUDENT VOICE

Self-reflections on inquiry learning

"My original question was, 'Is it true that eating processed meat is really that bad for me?' Then I realized that my question was leading me to only look for negative points about processed meat. So I changed it to 'What are the pros and cons of processed meat?' In my presentation, I was able to discuss reasons parents and kids like processed meat, as well as reasons why it is bad for your health. I felt confident doing this. In the end, I went back to the idea that processed meat is bad for you, but not so bad in moderation. The questions that I still have on this topic are: How is the production of processed meat impacting the environment? What kinds of actions are the big companies taking? Should government set stricter rules for big agri-companies?"

Aiden, Grade 8 student

"Something I liked about the inquiry was when I had to go on the internet to research about the topic. One thing I disliked about the inquiry was having to speak out loud in my group because I always get nervous. Something I can improve on is speaking out loud. Maybe I next time I can ask to work with a partner who makes me feel more comfortable because my group had all smart grade 8s and I feel like they judge me."

Ashwin, Grade 7 student

Attending to feelings

Reflection involves attending to feelings. In their research on reflection, David Boud et al. (1985) extended work done by John Dewey by identifying three components of effective reflection:

1. The learner returns to the experience (What did I do? What did I think? How did I feel?).

2. The learner attends to or connects with their feelings during the experience. They learn to identify and use positive feelings, and learn to identify and remove obstructive feelings.

3. The learner re-evaluates the experience in light of their intent and existing knowledge and gains new perspective. This new perspective may lead to action and future application of the new perspectives.

Boud's second component of reflection is often overlooked in classroom reflection. If a student does not connect to their feelings as they reflect on their experiences, they cannot identity feelings that support or inhibit their learning. Without attending to feelings, a student cannot modify their thinking to attend to the feelings. For example, a student who feels frustrated when asked to ask critical questions of a series of posts on a social media site needs to examine why they feel frustrated and what actions can they take to get over the frustration (i.e., ask a question, clarify the task, simplify the task, try it out and see how it goes).

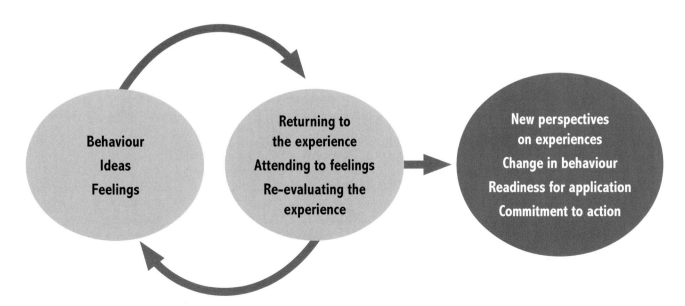

FIGURE 6.2 Boud's reflection cycle identifies three components of effective reflection.

Let's consider the practical application of Boud's reflection components in a typical classroom situation. Students have been practicing assessing sources from the Internet. The focus of a particular learning activity has been on determining the credibility of a source. The teacher has chosen in advance a list of five possible Internet sources on the inquiry question, "How does social media impact the mental health of teens?" Three of the sources are from highly credible organizations and authors, two are not. Students work in groups to determine the credibility of the sources. At the end of the activity, the teacher mediates student reflection by asking students to complete an exit card with the following questions:

- When you first saw the list of five Internet sources, which ones did you think were the most credible, least credible and why?

- After discussion with your group, how did your thinking about any of the Internet sources change? Why did it change?

- How did you feel when you were trying to assess your Internet sources on your own and in your group?

- How do these feelings help or challenge you?

- What could you do next time to help you effectively assess an Internet source for credibility?

- What could I, the teacher do next time to help you assess Internet sources?

These reflection questions ask the student to move through the three components of reflection. They remember their initial thinking (not an easy cognitive task); reconsider any changes in their thinking and why change may have occurred; identify feelings that are helpful and that may pose an obstacle to their thinking; and finally, envision future actions based on the reflective process. This exit card also provides assessment information for the teacher on how the student is doing in terms of their knowledge of assessing sources. More importantly, it provides an opportunity for students to think about how they learn and how they can change their behaviours, skills and attitudes in an effort to make themselves better learners.

Making reflection work for your students

Reflection works well when it is modelled by teacher and students and practiced on a regular basis. Reflections are most effective when students can see the impact of reflection in helping them to improve their skills and deepen their learning. It should also build confidence in intermediate learners. Reproducible 6A, *Why reflecting is awesome!* could be used to brainstorm positive effects of reflection in learning. Use the blank reproducible with students to generate an individual classroom account. Return to the reproducible over time as reflection skills improve.

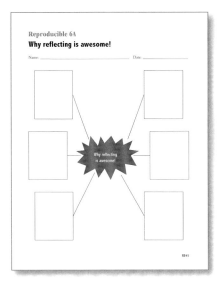

FIGURE 6.3 Reproducible 6A, p. RE45.

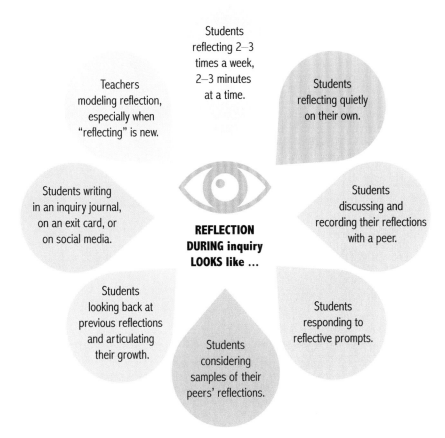

REFLECTION DURING inquiry LOOKS like ...

Students reflecting 2–3 times a week, 2–3 minutes at a time.

Teachers modeling reflection, especially when "reflecting" is new.

Students writing in an inquiry journal, on an exit card, or on social media.

Students looking back at previous reflections and articulating their growth.

Students considering samples of their peers' reflections.

Students reflecting quietly on their own.

Students discussing and recording their reflections with a peer.

Students responding to reflective prompts.

FIGURE 6.4 Reflection doesn't just happen. Teachers need to carve out time and space if it is to become a regular part of inquiry learning.

Check in with your learners and ask them what type of reflection activities and protocols they like best and the reasons for their preferences. It may be best to stick to two or three reflection protocols so that students become skilled and comfortable in their use. Make reflection as seamless as possible in your inquiry activities, and use oral and social media formats to increase student interest.

FIGURE 6.5 As students reflect during their inquiry, you should hear expressions of confusion, excitement, pride, rethinking, wondering, questioning and analysis.

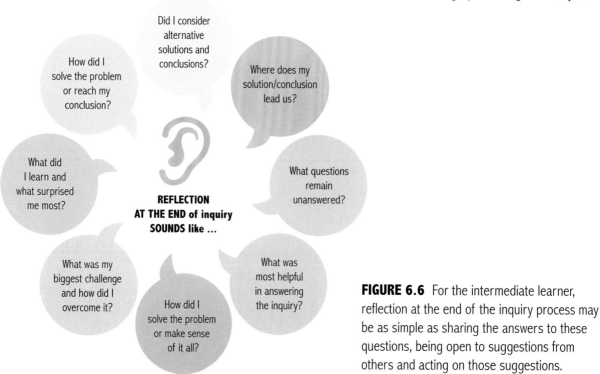

FIGURE 6.6 For the intermediate learner, reflection at the end of the inquiry process may be as simple as sharing the answers to these questions, being open to suggestions from others and acting on those suggestions.

Sharing at the end of an inquiry

Sharing the outcomes of an inquiry should be exciting. It is a time to celebrate your students' learning and to highlight their unique thinking, solutions and creations. It should also be a time of support because inquiry asks for a potentially humbling but helpful "double check" of thinking, solutions and creations by peers. Student work is not just "presented" as a static finished work; it becomes an invitation for others to get enthusiastic and curious about another learner's adventure to solve a problem or answer a question. Products of inquiry should be presented as a learner's thinking "up to this point" and as an invitation for others to engage. This highlights the fact that learning is an ongoing process and that conclusions change and evolve naturally as we learn more.

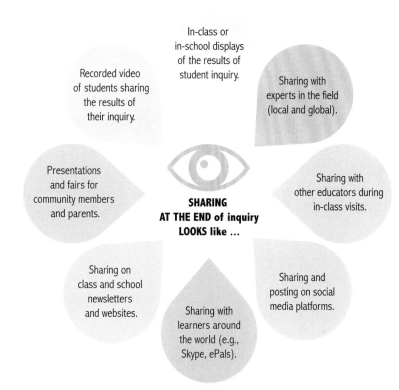

FIGURE 6.7 Sharing works best when teachers and schools create places, venues, connections and events specifically designed to help students share their inquiry work.

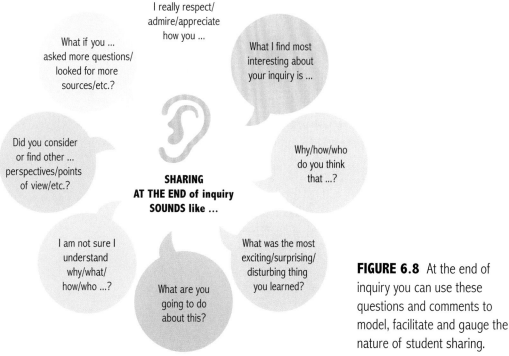

FIGURE 6.8 At the end of inquiry you can use these questions and comments to model, facilitate and gauge the nature of student sharing.

Some of the common terminology used for this endpoint of an inquiry method is "sharing findings," "taking action," "improving" and "checking and extending." What each of these terminologies share is the idea that the conclusions of the inquiry are open for consideration and can be further deepened through collaboration with other students as "learner-experts." These learner-experts help to ensure the quality of the product. Students are learner-experts when they understand and can apply the criteria of an effective inquiry. Students that have participated in the co-creation of criteria for an effective inquiry and have had multiple opportunities to self-assess and peer-assess are skilled learner-experts.

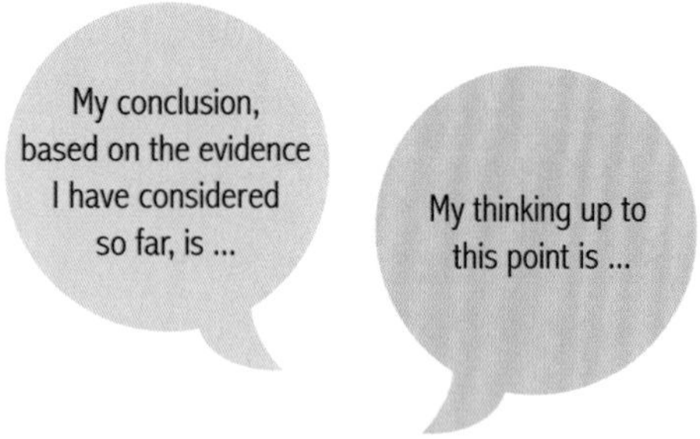

The sharing stage of an inquiry is an opportunity to highlight inquiry dispositions for your students. Students should be encouraged to demonstrate curiosity, wonder and open-mindedness towards the learning of their peers. They can once again question, critique and provide new perspectives. An important aim in the sharing stage is for students to be "amazed" at the new learning discovered by their peers and to learn more about themselves as learners while witnessing the learning of others.

THINQ

- How might your students benefit from more frequent opportunities for sharing and reflection?
- How might you overcome obstacles or barriers to building reflection and sharing into your classroom routines?
- How might you plan for the endpoint of one specific student inquiry to have more sharing and reflection?

My conclusion, based on the evidence I have considered so far, is ...

My thinking up to this point is ...

FIGURE 6.9 When conclusions are shared, they should be presented as a learner's thinking "up to this point" and as an invitation for others to engage. This highlights the fact that conclusions change and evolve as we learn more.

TECH-ENABLED INQUIRY

Sharing through technology

Intermediate students are often engaged by the idea of sharing their inquiry journey with a wider audience. Social media apps make it easy for students to connect with other students at various stages of an inquiry. There are countless free knowledge-sharing apps for students that can connect them to people with the same interests or to specific online communities. Some of these apps are website-building tools with simple and attractive interfaces. Other apps include large databases of general or themed information that is compiled, maintained and shared by an online user community. Many knowledge-sharing apps combine media clips, links and conversations that encourage others to participate in the discussion. Video sharing is another popular way to spread new knowledge resulting from inquiry learning.

6.3 How do I get students to give and respond to supportive critique?

BIG IDEA

Rich learning happens when students are expected to give and respond to supportive critique.

Intermediate students become (age-appropriate) experts in inquiry learning through experience, reflection and sharing. The endpoint of an inquiry cycle includes an important opportunity for collaborative, supportive and appreciative "critique." Sharing our inquiry work with others is not a one-way experience. Inquiry sharing involves the student presenting the journey that led to their final product and peers responding back in a meaningful way. The presenting student is then called on to consider the critique and improve the work.

CONTEXT

What are your intermediate learners' greatest strengths and challenges when it comes to giving and responding to critiques and feedback?

Supportive critique

This quality assurance and knowledge-building process is found in many disciplines and professions. Writers engage in supportive critique sessions with other writers where they "meet and critique." Chefs ask other chefs to test their food. Artists have exhibits judged by peers. Scientists and many other professions have their research peer-reviewed or refereed to decide if it is ready for publication in a scientific journal. Athletes have coaches or former athletes look at videotapes of their performance to advise on next steps for improvement. Students may have to be convinced that people learn together in this way in the "real world." Some students may be possessive or competitive with their knowledge and need to see knowledge in a new way — that is, as socially constructed and shared for positive purposes and action.

WORDS MATTER

Critique versus feedback

We have chosen to use the work *critique* instead of *feedback* to distinguish this as part of the endpoint stage of inquiry, as opposed to the ongoing feedback that is provided throughout all learning experiences, including inquiries.

INQUIRY IN ACTION

Developing frameworks for supportive critiques

Mr. Hill's class was investigating various inquiry questions regarding the lack of safe drinking water in First Nations communities in Ontario. Most students in the class were using animated presentations for their final product, but Matt and Elisha wanted to present a spoken word product. Mr. Hill worked through the success criteria for the final product with Matt and Elisha and asked them how these criteria should differ for a spoken word presentation. During peer critique time, peers were also asked what the criteria should be for a successful spoken word presentation. Mr. Hill now had a finalized assessment tool to use for Matt and Elisha's work and a potential framework for students who also would like to create a spoken word product in the future.

Supportive critique is an opportunity for students to negotiate the standards by which their work will be judged. Even if students have been co-constructors of the success criteria for an inquiry, sharing the work allows for initial success criteria to be modified and updated to reflect new realities of the learning and products at hand. For example, let's say that your students are creating different products to represent their inquiry learning. While the success criteria for inquiry processes may remain the same, unique success criteria may need to be developed, or previous success criteria honed to suit each learner's final product. Instead of attempting to create finalized assessment tools for each learner's product ahead of time, the process of supportive critique provides the perfect opportunity to develop valid and individualized assessment tools for final products.

CONVICTION
How do you feel about the notion that assessment plans and success criteria can be revised during the process to better reflect individual student needs and work?

Timing

Timing is everything in peer critique. It should occur near the end point of the inquiry process but allow time for students to respond to supportive suggestions regarding the process and product. Peer critique should not happen during a final presentation, since it is too late for the students to use the critique, although some other type of peer assessment may occur.

FIGURE 6.10 Even though many intermediate learners may be experienced at using feedback, it is always important to review how to effectively give and receive a critique.

Offering a critique	Receiving and responding to a critique
• Use anchor charts, rubrics and exemplars that detail the quality of work expected. • Be positive and enthusiastic; tell the person what is effective and what is interesting. • Ask for clarification if you are unsure. • Raise a concern, but be clear and specific. • Don't give too many suggestions (focus on what is most important to improving the work). • Don't change the person's work on their behalf (e.g., spelling, rewriting, corrections).	• Listen carefully. • Don't be defensive or get angry. • Respond to suggestions by explaining further. • Ask questions if you don't understand the suggestion. • Say thank you. • Take action on suggestions that you feel will most improve your work. • Be prepared to explain why you rejected suggestions (if you do).

Students should already be familiar with the norms of providing supportive feedback (i.e., positive body language, active listening, thanking the person for sharing, focusing on one or two criteria for change, asking clarifying questions, showing specific appreciation for the work). However, the protocol for the peer critique may differ depending on the product and the student's prior skill with inquiry learning. Reproducible 6B, *Criteria and advice for giving and receiving supportive critique* is a reminder to students on how to get the most out of a peer critique protocol. Reproducibles 6C, *Protocol for providing feedback: Building on what's good* and 6D, *Protocol for receiving feedback: Building on what's good* are places to record information as well as self-assessment tools for critique partners, or, as we like to call them, critique "buddies." Reproducible 6C is for the person providing a critique and Reproducible 6D is for the person whose work is being critiqued. Both reproducibles should be used together to record key points from the critique and to assess the role of both partners in the process.

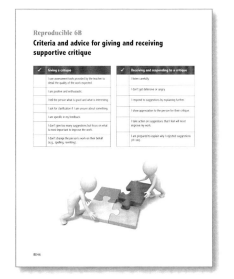

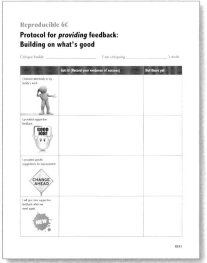

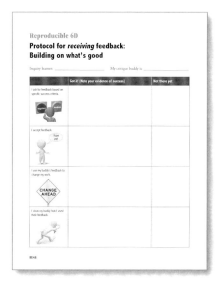

FIGURES 6.11–6.13 Reproducibles 6B, 6C and 6D, pp. RE46–RE48.

6.4 What are some practical tools to help students reflect and share?

Some teachers tell us that students do not enjoy reflection and sharing activities. This is often due to the fact that collaborative norms have not been co-created and supported. Without collaborative norms in place, students worry about being criticized during sharing activities. Similarly, students can be wary of reflection activities, seeing them as meaningless "add-ons" to learning activities. This is the case when the reflection activity is too onerous, lengthy, abstract or disconnected from the learning at hand.

We have observed classrooms where students are very excited and extremely involved in reflection and supportive sharing. Ask students which protocols they find most valuable (and enjoyable) and stick to those. Use role play, exemplars and personal narratives from your learning experiences to highlight the possibilities and challenges of reflection and sharing. When reflecting and sharing become the norm in your classroom, you'll have created a community of learners.

We have taken many of the suggestions made in this chapter and created Reproducibles 6E, 6F and 6G, which may help you incorporate more student sharing, critique and reflection. These templates do not have to be pencil-and-paper tasks. They can be used for interviews, digital reflections and ongoing conversations between students, and between students and teachers. You should modify these templates to better meet the needs of your students.

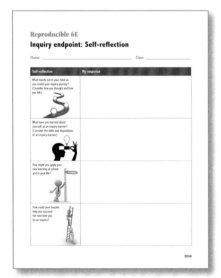

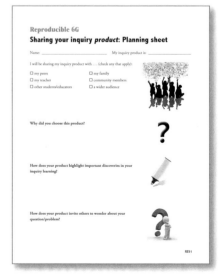

FIGURES 6.14–6.16 Reproducibles 6E, 6F and 6G, pp. RE49–RE51.

Using technology to support sharing and reflection

Technologies that support sharing and reflection can bring some added magic to this stage of the process. Some students may appreciate audio recording apps or vlogging for self- and peer-reflection. Reflections can be easily accessed in online storage sites (e.g., Dropbox). Collaboration in real-time is possible when creating and sharing reflections (including supportive critique) in blended learning platforms (e.g., Google Classroom). These sites and platforms are not only convenient; they allow students to see growth over time in their thinking and skill development.

Sharing inquiry products with authentic audiences is easy and exciting through the use of social media apps. Students can connect with other students and experts at various stages of an inquiry. Many knowledge-sharing apps combine media clips, links and conversations that encourage others to participate in the discussion.

We encourage all teachers to become proficient with several applications that support the pedagogical aims of student sharing and reflection. Don't worry about becoming an expert in the applications — your students will get you there.

TECH-ENABLED INQUIRY

Recommended reflection and sharing apps

There is an endless proliferation of educational apps to refresh and support inquiry learning tasks. Below is a list of popular and effective apps used in classrooms.

Tech that supports inquiry product sharing

- **iMovie:** Movie-making app
- **Animoto:** Video and photo slideshow maker
- **GoAnimate:** Animated video creator
- **PowToon:** Animated presentations and videos
- **Book Creator:** Create and publish e-books
- **Comic Life:** Turn photos into a comic book
- **Keynote:** Make "gorgeous" presentations
- **Haiku Deck:** Create "beautiful" presentations
- **Pinterest:** Content sharing via "pin boards" of photos and websites
- **Voki:** Create customizable avatars for class presentations
- **Youth Voices:** Blog sharing for young people

Tech that supports inquiry process sharing

- **Google Classroom:** Productivity tools for classroom collaboration
- **Edmodo:** Blended-learning classroom
- **Educreations:** Interactive whiteboard
- **Explain Everything:** Interactive and collaborative whiteboard
- **Mixed Ink:** Collaborative policy writing
- **Voki:** Avatar creator with voice-recording features
- **Audacity:** Cross-platform audio software
- **Twitter:** Social network
- **Facebook:** Social network
- **Padlet:** Virtual bulletin board
- **Popplet:** Collaborative mind-mapping

Revisit and reflect

This chapter made the argument that it is important to build in frequent opportunities for sharing, critique and reflection throughout the inquiry process, including the final stage of the inquiry process.

You were asked to consider the benefits of sharing, critique and reflection for student learning. We explored what sharing and reflection look and sound like in the classroom, and we provided some practical strategies to help students become better at critiquing others' work and reflecting on their own learning.

In the next chapter, we examine the big ideas of inquiry that underpin a successful inquiry-based learning program and provide a planning model that has helped many teachers integrate more inquiry into their teaching and assessment practice.

BIG IDEAS

6.1 Inquiry learning becomes deep learning through reflection and sharing.

6.2 Students and teachers need concrete examples of what good reflection and sharing look and sound like.

6.3 Rich learning happens when students are expected to give and respond to supportive critique.

6.4 Collaborative norms are essential to maximize the power and effectiveness of reflecting and sharing in inquiry learning.

THINQ

- How might sharing, critique and reflection help push your students' learning and thinking to a deeper level?

- What is missed if teachers do not find the time to build sharing and reflection opportunities into each stage of the inquiry process, including the final stage of the process?

- How could you harness technology to support student reflection, critique and sharing?

Chapter 7
WRAPPING IT UP:
What matters most

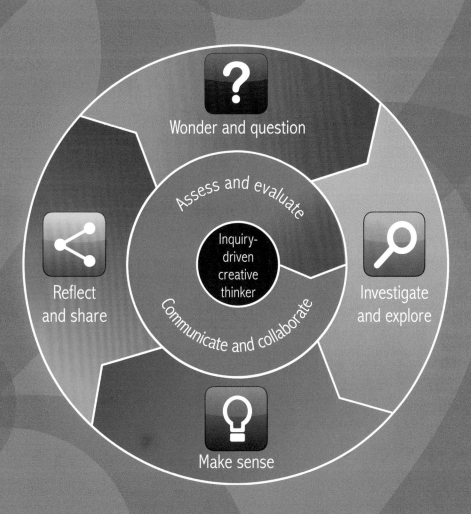

Wonder and question

Assess and evaluate

Inquiry-driven creative thinker

Reflect and share

Investigate and explore

Communicate and collaborate

Make sense

7.1 What are the big ideas of inquiry?

THINQ 7–9: Inquiry-based learning in the intermediate classroom has been written specifically for educators of intermediate learners — students in grades 7 to 9. We have argued that inquiry-based learning can capitalize on the curiosity and growing intellectual skill that naturally reside in young adult learners.

Inquiry-based learning has a long theoretical history in education, but it has not been implemented in a systematic, integrated way in most schools and districts. We believe it is possible to do so. We believe this book can help.

THINQ 7–9 identifies the big ideas that underpin a successful inquiry-based learning program and provides practical strategies for planning, instruction and assessment within this framework. To conclude this book, we summarize the twenty-five biggest ideas at the core of inquiry-based learning and present a ten-step model to plan for and do more inquiry.

Twenty-five big ideas about inquiry-based learning

In this section you'll find twenty-five big ideas that are we feel are at the core of inquiry-based learning. These ideas were explored throughout *THINQ 7–9* and represent the enduring understandings of this resource and pedagogy. You'll notice that they aren't organized around the stages of the inquiry process. This isn't because we believe that inquiry process models aren't useful, but rather that big ideas apply regardless of inquiry stage, discipline, grade level or educational environment. You may want to use these big ideas with your teaching partners, staff or senior administrators to plan for more inquiry in teaching and assessment programs.

❶ We learn by asking questions (inquiring).

Inquiry learning is rooted in our innate desire to make sense of the mysterious world. When we ask questions, determine a problem, and use our heads and hearts to investigate what fascinates us, we are engaged in inquiry.

2 **Inquiry dispositions grow through a supportive classroom community that supports everyone's creativity and critical thought.**

Curiosity, open-mindedness and confidence in your ability to reason are inquiry dispositions. They are what keeps the learner on the journey of inquiry. These dispositions support risk-taking and commitment to inquiry learning. They make us perseverant and accepting of failure and mistakes as an important part of the journey. A safe, inviting, engaging and collaborative classroom makes growth in inquiry dispositions possible.

3 **All knowledge is living and changing because it is personally and socially constructed.**

Students learn best when they are invited to be part of the active and exciting process of knowledge building. Learners are no longer viewed as containers to be filled with disconnected bits of knowledge; they are naturally curious, rational and committed to making sense of their world. Teachers also teach best when they are intellectually engaged in their craft and not merely following lock-step curricular or instructional mandates.

4 **All inquiry learning, regardless of grade or discipline, has three common essential traits.**

All inquiry learning experiences share three traits: an essential question that invites the learner to wonder, think deeply and solve; answering the question or solving the problem using a method or process; and thinking critically, self-reflecting, contributing, communicating and sharing findings so that new knowledge is created.

Curiosity
Eagerness to learn
or know something

Criticality
Objective analysis
and evaluation

Hopefulness
Feeling or inspiring
optimism about
the future

Open-mindedness
Willingness to
consider new ideas

FIGURE 7.1 Inquiry dispositions

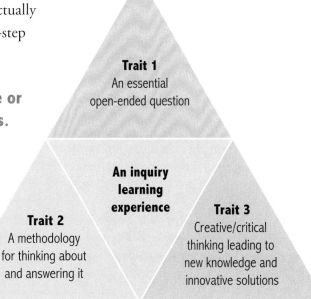

Trait 1
An essential
open-ended question

An inquiry
learning
experience

Trait 2
A methodology
for thinking about
and answering it

Trait 3
Creative/critical
thinking leading to
new knowledge and
innovative solutions

FIGURE 7.2 Essential traits of inquiry learning

⑤ Central to inquiry learning are beliefs about who learners are and what they are capable of.

Inquiry learning encourages human curiosity. It demands rational thought and ethical considerations. It is grounded in what is already known, but pushes the learner to add to this knowledge through a process in which they explore the ideas again from new perspectives and viewpoints. Learners are in control. They are active participants, not passive recipients. Learning is a collaborative endeavour.

⑥ Inquiry learning is a continuum, with guided inquiry and a large degree of teacher direction at one end, and open inquiry with a large degree of student autonomy at the other.

Open-inquiry is the long-term goal. Teacher-directed and blended inquiry are practical classroom realities. A teacher's decision about the balance between teacher direction and student autonomy in an inquiry will depend on their assessment of the conditions in their classroom and the capacity and experience of their students.

FIGURE 7.3 Moving from guided to open inquiry

⑦ At the heart of assessment are teachers and students asking, "How are we doing?"

Assessment, in a fundamental way, is about teachers and students pausing to reflect independently on the question, "How am I doing?" and collectively, "How are we doing?" These questions relate to both academic and social-emotional learning. They allow us to consider our aims as individual learners and to empower and improve learning. Six essential abilities are at the core of inquiry activities and assessment.

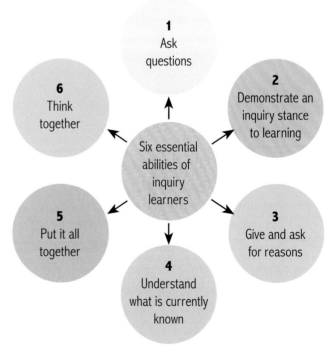

FIGURE 7.4 The essential abilities of inquiry learners

8 Curriculum should be seen not as the end, but as the means to engage students in rich learning activities.

Curriculum should be regarded as a means, not an end. If our aim is for students to engage in rich, personally- and socially-significant learning activities that target big ideas and enduring understandings, then the items that make up curriculum become the means and context to carry out this learning. However, a desire to cover every aspect of the curriculum in detail will likely restrict your ability to plan and implement inquiry-based learning.

9 Students should be our assessment partners.

Students should have a say in what to aim for, what quality looks like, and how to demonstrate their learning. Authentic snapshots of learning are not just possible, but practical with new handheld technologies that allow students to capture their thinking to share with peers, teachers and parents. Inquiry assessment is an iterative three-stage process that involves gathering, interpreting and responding to evidence of a student's inquiry skills and dispositions.

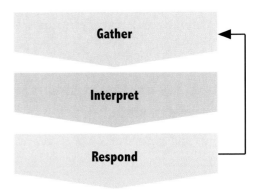

FIGURE 7.5 The inquiry assessment process

10 Our curiosity fuels our learning.

Inquiry begins with wondering. Learning begins with questions. We are all curious about the way the world works. Our curiosity fuels and gives purpose to our learning. We can sense when wonder is at work in our students — they are fascinated and focused. Questions arise. Creativity and critical thinking abound. At these moments, the learner feels excited and determined to dive deeper into their learning.

11 The purpose of an inquiry question is to entice your students to think deeply about the mysteries of life.

Inquiry questions are helpful to learners because they stimulate thinking and feeling, and they drive learning by signalling what is truly essential and fascinating about their world. They can often be deceptively simple, but they cannot be simply answered.

12 **Questions that elicit strong emotions are often the best place to begin.**

Often teachers and students aren't sure about whether their questions are "good" questions. One key criterion of a good inquiry question is whether it evokes strong emotions and feelings. If the question generates debate and controversy, you've likely got yourself a good question.

13 **High engagement improves student achievement.**

Inquiry learning demands student engagement both intellectually and emotionally. When students are internally motivated to solve a problem, student achievement (based on inquiry learning outcomes) is positively impacted.

14 **We need to describe exactly what good thinking involves and encourage students to be attentive to their own thinking.**

Inquiry-based learning requires considerable amounts of reasoning. We can't just ask students to "think harder" — we need to describe exactly what good thinking involves and encourage students to be attentive to their own thinking, even when we are not there prompting them to do so. Teaching them how to avoid common "thinking traps" and how to use specific "thinking boosts" helps achieve the goal of good thinking.

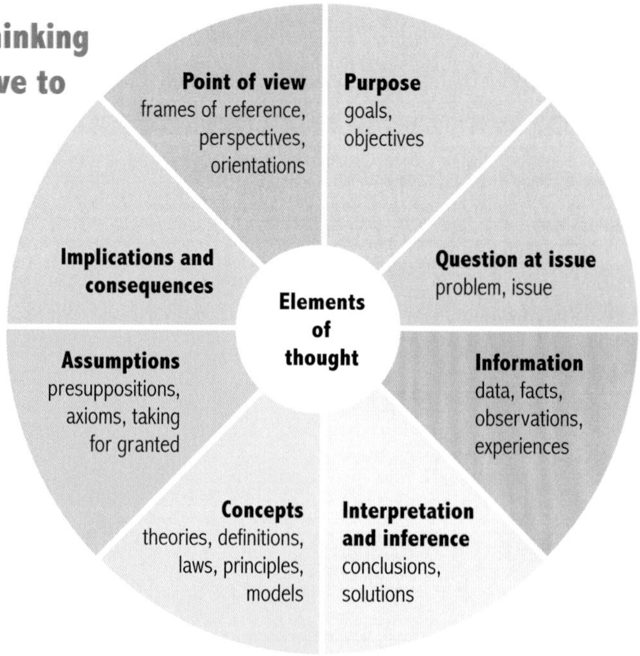

15 **Teachers need to help students become better questioners.**

Questioning is a crucial inquiry skill and is found in each method of inquiry and at each stage of every model. Students need to be explicitly taught how to develop good questions and become good questioners. This requires the development and application of success criteria for good questions.

16 **Constructing a rich response to a question is more appealing when students know there is no predetermined "correct" answer.**

Too often when we give students a question to answer, our expectation is that they should "get the right answer." Getting the "right answer" doesn't often require deep thinking, since students rarely encounter anything that is debatable or inconclusive.

FIGURE 7.6 The eight elements of thought

However, it is the debatable points of life that are often the most interesting and stimulating. We need to engage students by asking them to investigate questions that have many valid and sometimes contradictory answers.

17 Teachers need to be both leaders of and co-learners alongside their students.

It is good for students to see that their teachers don't have all the answers. No one does! And if the answers are already known, then what learning really takes place in the investigation of those questions? Rote learning and memorization may show short-term results, but these are very different from the consequences of deep thinking. As students gain more experience with inquiry and develop their inquiry skills, and as teachers gain more experience facilitating inquiry-based learning, the role of the teacher will naturally evolve to meet the unique needs of students from year to year.

18 Teachers need to model an inquiry stance as well as provide parameters and structures to ensure student success.

Teachers should support students during the inquiry process by planning to uncover preconceived ideas and misconceptions, locating a selection of age- and grade-appropriate sources from a variety of perspectives, and helping students assess the credibility of sources.

19 When we synthesize a body of information, we gain new knowledge.

The creation of new knowledge often, but not exclusively, comes after a body of evidence is synthesized or consolidated. Synthesis, or what we call "making sense" for intermediate learners, like other elements of thinking and learning, needs to be taught explicitly.

20 Students must reflect on their assumptions or biases.

At all stages of inquiry learning, students must consider how to strengthen their thinking by considering their own assumptions and biases. Whether developing a question (questions are never neutral), selecting sources, or analyzing sources, biases influence reasoning. Students can learn to actively question their beliefs, consider alternative views and update topic knowledge.

FIGURE 7.7 A visual metaphor for synthesis

21 **Students benefit from watching us model how to organize notes and cite sources.**

Some intermediate students believe that cutting and pasting from the Internet is research. Direct teaching of the skills of organizing notes and properly citing sources will benefit them in their academic and professional futures.

22 **Sound conclusions can be drawn only after a body of evidence is carefully weighed.**

At the most basic level, drawing a conclusion is really about weighing the evidence. Most inquiries will have a number of "branches" of exploration and associated evidence. Only after students have consolidated their evidence can they begin to effectively draw conclusions or develop solutions.

23 **Metacognition deepens learning.**

When students are asked to pause and intentionally consider their "inner voice" or cognitive processes, this is metacognition. Metacognition can increase a learner's self-awareness of their strengths, limitations in learning and the strategies and tools that they use in their thinking. Being aware of the process of your learning makes you a better learner.

24 **Deep learning and understanding results from reflection and discussion with others.**

Teachers can push learning to a deeper level by having students reflect on their thinking, feelings and conclusions, sharing with others, and then reflecting again. The reflection and sharing process in an inquiry is really the same as best practice assessment *for* and *as* learning, so this is not a new type of pedagogy.

25 **Inquiry should involve empathy.**

Empathy asks that we consider the feelings and needs of others as we inquire. Empathy is ideally both a shared feeling *and* an accurate understanding of another person's experiences and beliefs. Empathy is an honest attempt to "walk in the shoes" of others before we answer a question or solve a problem that impacts those very people.

CAPACITY
Which of these big ideas are already part of your teaching and assessment practices?

COMMITMENT
Which of these big ideas would you like to incorporate into your practice?

7.2 How do I move forward from here?

Many new curriculum guidelines and school board directives are embracing inquiry-based learning as a key objective. We believe this is because inquiry-based learning is a bridge to successful teaching and learning in the digital age. It will be well worth the investment to build your capacity to work within an inquiry-based learning framework.

In our work with teachers, we found that many have little time to read professional learning resources, especially if those resources are not built into a professional learning program. If both professional development days within our school boards and time to read about pedagogy and instruction are limited, then how do we move our professional skills forward?

We suggest you plan your first inquiry with the big ideas in mind. If you plan according to the big ideas of inquiry, then rich learning will happen regardless of whether or not the inquiry itself "goes" the way you originally imagined. There are a number of ways to plan an inquiry, but we have sketched out one approach that has proven successful for many teachers.

① Start with a guided inquiry.

We suggest you begin with a guided inquiry. There is lots of time for your students to conduct their own student-driven inquiries *after* they have experience and expertise with inquiry-based learning. We believe that starting with guided-inquiry is the best way to create the conditions that lead to student success.

② Determine your broad curricular targets.

All inquiries are about something and it's up to you to decide which area of the curriculum you want to target. Make sure you are working from broad curricular targets (sometimes called "overall expectations" or "overarching targets" in curriculum guidelines) rather than the list of small, specific expectations that so often fill curriculum guidelines. Working from broad curriculum targets will give students choice within the inquiry experience you design. Remember that you can choose curriculum targets from different curriculum areas to build a great inquiry that bridges language arts, social studies and science, for example.

10 steps to doing more inquiry

1. Start with a guided inquiry.

2. Determine your broad curricular targets.

3. Develop rich inquiry questions from your targets.

4. Create an assessment plan.

5. Locate and collect grade- and age-appropriate sources to drive the inquiry.

6. Build in opportunities for ongoing sharing and reflection (including metacognitive reflection).

7. Create and reinforce vocabulary to communicate inquiry thinking.

8. Help students make sense of the evidence.

9. Assist students in drawing conclusions based on their evidence.

10. Include time to reflect on and share conclusions.

FIGURE 7.8

3 Develop rich inquiry questions from your targets.

For inquiry-based learning to work effectively, students must start with an inquiry question that is both exciting and focused on the big ideas of a discipline. All effective inquiry questions have certain characteristics. You may choose to have the entire class work together on one inquiry question, or have groups of students investigate three or four questions looking at different aspects of the curriculum targets you have selected.

4 Create an assessment plan.

Assessment bridges teaching and learning. It identifies where the learner is going (by establishing and sharing big ideas, concepts, fundamental skills, related learning goals and success criteria); where the learner is right now in their learning (by observing students, having conversations and assessing products); and how to get the learner to their goal (through the use of peer, self- and teacher feedback).

An assessment plan is a map of when and how you will purposefully analyze student work throughout the inquiry process. An assessment plan also includes how you plan to evaluate inquiry skills and other curriculum outcomes that you have identified as crucial to student learning in a specific inquiry.

Remember that the burden of assessment doesn't fall to you alone. Students need to be partners in the assessment process by providing peer feedback and reflecting and reporting on their own learning.

5 Locate and collect grade- and age-appropriate sources to drive the inquiry.

Assembling a set of inquiry resources for your students can feel like a burden, which is why teachers sometimes continue on with what they have always done. We want to stress that building a "starter" set of resources to drive inquiry in your classroom is well worth it. It will ensure that students consider resources with a variety of perspectives and increase the chances they will have an enjoyable and successful inquiry experience. Even better, since a

An effective inquiry question...	
1 ... is an invitation to think (not recall, summarize or detail).	**2** ... comes from genuine curiosity and/or confusion about the world.
3 ... makes you think about something in a way you haven't before.	**4** ... invites both deep thinking and deep feelings.
5 ... leads to more good questions.	**6** ... asks you to think about the essential ideas in a discipline.

FIGURE 7.9 Qualities of effective inquiry questions

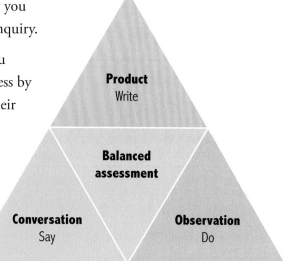

FIGURE 7.10 Elements of balanced assessment

rich question will lead to any number of valid, evidence-based conclusions, you will be able to use the source collection over many years and your digitally-savvy students will help add to this dynamic collection.

6 Build in opportunities for ongoing collaboration, sharing and reflection (including metacognitive reflection).

One of the fundamental qualities of inquiry is that students work together to make sense of a question or problem. Outside of school, we rarely learn in isolation and few of us work at jobs where we function completely independently. Plan on having students work together at least some of the time.

The inquiry process also demands regular opportunities for students to discuss and reflect on their learning, and to loop back to reconsider, revise and/or restructure their thoughts. Adjusting students' workloads to provide more time for reflection, especially metacognitive reflection, increases the chances that students will come to understand more about not only the inquiry at hand, but about themselves and their classmates as thinkers and learners.

7 Create and reinforce vocabulary to communicate inquiry thinking.

Communication is the way that students make their learning visible. Effective communication requires the integration of inquiry vocabulary into your daily classroom tasks. Over time, you should notice a new and powerful common language being spoken by your students. This will accelerate their ability to move towards independent inquiry. The strategies in Figure 7.11 will help you to develop such a vocabulary amongst your students.

8 Help students make sense of the evidence.

Whether you provide a full or partial bundle of sources for your students, or have students gather their own evidence, you will need to teach them how to make sense of their data. This includes helping them to consider the quality, reliability, usefulness and perspective of their sources and of their thinking.

Strategies for building inquiry vocabulary

- Create anchor charts or word walls of key inquiry vocabulary.

- Have students complete an inquiry journal where they articulate their understanding of new inquiry vocabulary as it arises.

- When listening to collaborative groups, ask questions that invite students to explain their understanding of key inquiry vocabulary in relation to the work they are completing.

- Students can create T-charts, Venn diagrams or other key visuals to define key inquiry vocabulary words, or to compare two or more key inquiry vocabulary words.

- Have inquiry vocabulary "check-ins" by asking students comprehension and application questions. You can create the questions, or even better, have students create the questions on specific terms to assess their peers.

FIGURE 7.11

9 Assist students in drawing conclusions based on their evidence.

Help your students draw conclusions by having them identify patterns and trends, and reflect on the quality of evidence. Remember, a key goal of inquiry is for students to understand that their conclusions should be based on their analysis of evidence within an ethical framework. Another student working from the same sources may come up with an entirely different evidence-based conclusion. This is to be encouraged, and it will be a sign that the inquiry question was rich and powerful.

10 Include time to reflect on and share conclusions.

It seems counter-intuitive to us that after a period of rich learning, students would keep their learning to themselves. We advocate that students share and reflect on their learning throughout the inquiry process and also share and critique each other's work at the conclusion of the inquiry. This pushes learning to a deeper level. It promotes the idea that learning is an ongoing process and that discussion can always lead to a different conclusion.

Remember that inquiry-based learning in your classroom will look and sound very different over time as both you and your students develop more expertise and experience with inquiry. At some point your classroom will function very differently than it does now, and you and your students will be excited to come to school (most days!).

THINQ BIG

Teachers as inquiring professionals

We believe that teachers are powerful and effective researchers of their own practice. Teachers who are confident about their impact on the lives of their students and are curious and intentional about how to improve their practice are inquiry learners. It is exciting to see that in many classrooms, students are involved in inquiry learning while teaching partners, grade teams or entire staff are simultaneously involved in professional inquiries.

Teacher inquiry has the same qualities as student inquiry. It begins with a rich inquiry question such as, "What happens when we ask students to self-reflect on their reasoning?" Teacher inquiries should avoid cause-and-effect statements that "close" the inquiry. Notice the difference in the first statement and the two questions that follow:

1. If we provide self-reflection time, then students will become better learners.
2. What happens when we provide intentional scaffolding and metacognitive prompts for students to reflect on their questioning skills?
3. How can we model reasoning so that students understand weak and strong reasoning, can identify it, and can apply this understanding in their future learning?

Teacher inquiry begins with a rich inquiry question based on student learning needs and professional curiosity, and moves through an iterative and collaborative cycle of plan, act, document and reflect. Sharing the results of professional inquiries leads to further questions, and the inquiry cycle begins again. As teachers engage in professional inquiry, they could articulate their wonderings, reasoning, assumptions and biases, analysis and conclusions with their intermediate students. Students will be intrigued to see how adult learners are experiencing similar opportunities and challenges in inquiry learning as they are in their own learning.

You can read more about teacher collaborative inquiry in Jenni Donohoo's book *Collaborative Inquiry for Educators*.

REPRODUCIBLES

Reproducible 1A
The inquiry process

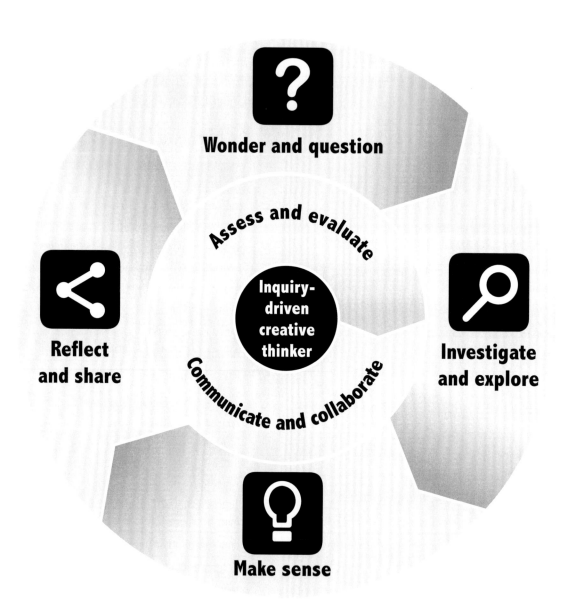

Reproducible 1B
Student exploration: What is inquiry?

Name: _____ Date: _____

Inquiry is a method of thinking that helps us to ask and answer deep and complex questions and solve important problems.

1. Which of the following do you think is a deep question or problem? Explain why you think so.

    a. Should I go to my friend's house after school today?

    b. How can we make our school more eco-friendly?

    c. How can we make a better smartphone?

    d. What is 150 ÷ 5?

    e. What is the capital of Canada?

    _____

    _____

2. State an example of a deep/complex question that interests you.

    _____

    _____

    _____

3. What makes some questions easier to answer than others?

    _____

    _____

4. What do you think you might have to do in order to answer a deep question or problem in an effective way?

    _____

    _____

Reproducible 1C
Student exploration: Curiosity is key

Name: _____ Date: _____

Have you ever wondered how something got to be a certain way, why people act the way they do, how something works, or how you could make something better?

If so, you have one of the most important qualities of an inquiry learner — you are curious!

Think about yourself as an inquiry learner by answering the following questions:

1. What makes you curious?

   _____

   _____

2. What do you feel like when you are curious?

   _____

   _____

3. Do you think it's important to be curious about the world? Why?

   _____

   _____

4. In what ways do your parents, caregivers, teachers and friends encourage your curiosity?

   _____

   _____

5. Is it possible to be bored if you are a curious person? Why or why not?

   _____

   _____

Reproducible 1D
Student exploration: I'm an inquiry learner!

Name: _____ Date: _____

An inquiry learner enjoys wondering about the world, asking and answering questions and solving problems.

- They like to discover, create, improve and innovate.
- They enjoy playing with ideas.
- They are open-minded to the ideas of others.
- They are not afraid of making mistakes.
- They don't give up on learning.
- They seek the ideas of others but don't accept everything they hear, see or read.
- They want to know more.

Thinking about the description of an inquiry learner above, complete the following statements:

1. I am an inquiry learner because...

   _____

   _____

2. My goal in becoming a better inquiry learner is...

   _____

   _____

3. My teacher and fellow students could help me become a better inquiry learner by...

   _____

   _____

Conversation cards: Let's talk about inquiry

Use the questions on these cards to engage in discussions on inquiry and inquiry dispositions with students.

When have you been engaged most as a learner and why?	**What makes you curious?**
Is it possible to be bored if you are a curious person? Why or why not?	**What does it mean to you to be an inquiry learner?**
How do your parents, friends and teachers encourage your curiosity?	**What does it mean to be a change agent?**
Share a time when you considered a different perspective.	**Is inquiry a better way to learn?**
What do you think you need in order to be successful with inquiry-based learning?	**What ways do you learn best?**

Teacher self-assessment: Inquiry readiness checklist

Check which of the following statements represents your knowledge, beliefs and understanding of inquiry learning. Use this checklist for self-reflection, for planning and sharing with colleagues, and to determine next steps in deepening your inquiry practice.

Conviction

- I believe in the main assumptions of inquiry-based learning: that learning is constructivist, student-centred and demands critical thinking.
- I am familiar with and convinced by the research that supports inquiry to improve student engagement and learning.

Commitment

- I am committed to bringing more inquiry-based learning to my classroom and have reflected on not only what makes me excited about inquiry learning, but also what makes me uncertain.
- I have connected with other committed educators who are interested in and supportive of inquiry education.

Capacity

- I understand that inquiry is a process used to answer questions, solve problems and make new knowledge.
- I understand that a guided inquiry is a highly-structured and thoughtfully designed endeavour that allows for optimal student autonomy.
- I know there are distinct stages involved in an inquiry process.
- I understand that there are many inquiry models to choose from but that these models share essential traits.
- I understand that inquiries are on a continuum from guided to open (and that a degree of guidance is essential for effective student learning).

Context

- I understand what my role should be in an inquiry classroom.
- I accept that inquiry learning in my classroom should be a "playful," "messy," complex, recursive, iterative, non-linear experience and not merely a lock-step process to completing a product.
- I have thought about my students' readiness for inquiry and know where to start.

Confirmation

- I know what my professional goals are with respect to doing more inquiry.
- I understand how I will assess my progress, what is working and how to improve.

Reproducible 2A

How to model and assess inquiry dispositions

Name: _____ Date: _____

Inquiry disposition	What it looks like in a classroom	How inquiry-based learning supports this disposition	Student reflection prompts
Curiosity and wonder	Teachers and students want to know more about the world and its people. They ask important, deep relevant questions. These questions are not answered easily - nor does the teacher or student have the correct answer in mind at the outset. They are honestly perplexed by an issue/question/problem and have the motivation to uncover a possible answer/solution.	Inquiry-based learning begins with a question, a curiosity or a wondering related to the discipline.	*An important question that I find interesting is …* *I think it is important to answer this question because …* *The question is hard to answer because …* *I feel I'm becoming a better questioner because …*
Criticality	Teacher and students enjoy the challenge of thinking deeply. Teacher and students trust that they can figure out difficult problems by using their reason and intelligence. Teacher and students are willing to try out different types of thinking (i.e., critical, creative, reflective) and different points of view.	Inquiry-based learning proceeds when learners trust that they can harness their own skills of reasoning when confronted with a challenging question. Inquiry-based learning allows students to develop discipline-specific thinking skills as they collect, critically assess and evaluate sources and then generate conclusions.	*Even though I may make mistakes, I believe I can succeed in this inquiry because …* *When confronted with a problem I cannot answer at first, I feel that …* *I have used critical thinking in this inquiry to …* *The thinking skill I have found most helpful in this inquiry is …*
Hopefulness	Teacher and students see the world as it is and like to think about how it can be improved. They care about and have a sense of purpose and commitment in their inquiries.	Inquiry-based learning is future oriented and involves problem-solving. It encourages students to create and share new knowledge and to be change agents.	*I think solving this problem is important because …* *I think I can solve this problem because …* *I think my ideas could make a difference because …* *This is how I went about making new knowledge …*
Open-mindedness	Teacher and students are genuinely interested in other perspectives and attitudes. They realize that the question is never fully answered and that knowledge is always being constructed. They are open to continual learning.	Inquiry-based learning demands that evidence and information is gathered from multiple sources that represent diverse perspectives. Inquiry-based learning is an adventure. It is typically not a linear process, but one with twists and turns. These intellectual surprises allow students to experience what true experts in the discipline feel when attempting to solve a problem.	*Different sources and points of view are important to consider in this inquiry because …* *The one perspective I am having difficulty understanding or finding evidence to support is …*

SOURCE: Adapted from J. Walsh and B. Sattes, *Thinking Through Quality Questioning*, Corwin Press (2011).

The six essential inquiry abilities for assessment

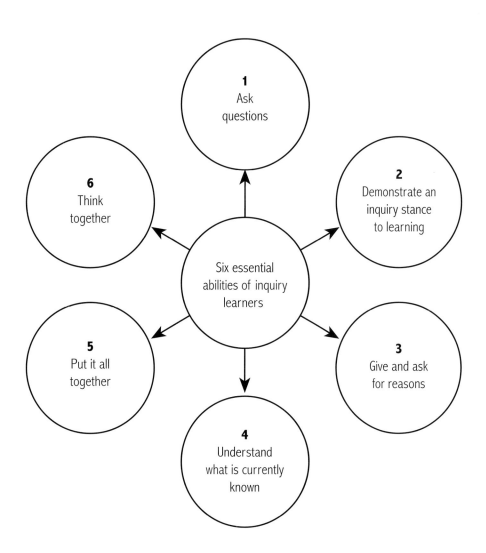

Student exploration: Who is an inquiry learner?

Name: _____ Date: _____

An inquiry is a way to go about solving an important problem or answering an important question. The following case study is an example of a problem that needs a solution.

Class 7B is having difficulty these days. There are two computers in the classroom and arguments result when more than two students want to use them for classwork.

Consider the comments made by students in Class 7B regarding this problem. Decide which of these students may be demonstrating the qualities of an inquiry learner and be prepared to explain your answer.

A. How are we supposed to figure this out — it's impossible! It's up to the teacher to fix the problem.

B. Let's do some math and figure out what might be a workable way to get computer time for everyone.

C. Can't we buy more computers instead of the new sports equipment?

F. Let's take the computers from the front office. Problem solved!

D. We should ask the principal, our parents, and other teachers for their advice before we make a decision.

E. It's not a problem for me. I can do my work on my home computer.

I. Just because everyone likes using the computer doesn't mean they really need it. Let's talk about what is really essential to do on the computer versus what is convenient or fun to do. Then we could create a schedule based on need.

G. Let's create a point system. Whoever wins the most points gets the most computer time.

H. The school should allow us to bring our own devices. I wonder who may object to that and why, and who would support this idea and why.

An inquiry rubric: What are the specific characteristics of a successful inquiry?

Name: _____   Date: _____

Areas that need work	Success criteria categories	How work exceeds expectations
	Inquiry skills and processes The student will: • Ask and refine relevant questions that further inquiry • Investigate and explore sources that suggest answers and solutions • Make sense of the evidence and draw logical conclusions	
	Application of thinking skills The student will: • Use critical, creative and discipline-related thinking skills in order to provide an answer or course of action	
	Communicate new understandings The student will: • Communicate clearly and persuasively engage the audience • Use the vocabulary and terminology of the discipline	
	Learn what is currently known about the question/problem The student will: • Demonstrate knowledge and understanding of content important to the inquiry	

Reproducible 2E

Assessment planning template: Asks questions

Name: _____ Date: _____

Essential inquiry ability — Asking questions	Evidence gathered		
	Conversations	Observations	Products
Asks questions • Asks and refines relevant questions for different purposes (to get information, to clarify, to dispute, to drive an inquiry) and from different perspectives.			
Demonstrates curiosity • Actively asks many questions that demonstrate eagerness to learn. • Understands the importance of questioning to learning.			
(Gives and) Asks for reasons • Asks for justification of beliefs, proposals and solutions. • Thinks together. • Listens to, builds on, considers and assists with the questions of others. • Asks relevant questions of other people to further an inquiry (to get an opinion or some advice, to debate, to dispute, to inquire, to brainstorm).			
Understands what is currently known • Asks critical questions of "what is already known" (i.e., sources, data, strategies, theories).			
Puts it all together • Asks and understands the importance of analytical questions to improve their thinking at each stage of an inquiry.			

Reproducible 2F
Essential inquiry vocabulary

Inquiry action words

Analyze	Examine something in detail
Assess	Consider the quality of something
Clarify	Make something easier to understand
Conclude	Decide something after thinking or research
Defend	Speak in favour of a person or idea
Explore	Look at something in a careful way to learn more about it
Evaluate	Judge something based on certain criteria
Investigate	Discover and examine facts to discover the truth
Make sense	Come to a logical explanation or understanding
Persuade	Convince someone of your way of thinking
Question	Request information or an answer
Reflect	Think deeply about something or someone
Refute	Prove something is wrong
Share	Give something to or experience something with others

Important inquiry concepts

Assumption	A belief something is true although there is no proof
Bias	Favouritism for or against something or someone
Curiosity	Desire to learn more about something
Feedback	Information that is used for the basis of improvement
Flexible	Willing to change or try different things
Implication	Possible effect or result of an action
Inquiry	Asking about and investigating questions and problems
Metacognition	Thinking about thinking, knowing about knowing
Open-minded	Willing to consider different ideas and opinions
Perspective	Mental view or outlook
Perseverance	Continuing to try even though it is difficult
Point of view	Particular attitude or way of thinking
Risk	Possibility something will fail
Self-confidence	Confidence in your powers and abilities
Wonder	Surprise caused by something beautiful, unfamiliar or inexplicable

Words to describe thoughts, feelings and beliefs

Abstract	Not a physical object, typically an idea
Accurate	Correct and true
Clear	Easy to understand, not confusing
Coherent	Logical and consistent
Concept	An idea of what something is or how it works
Effective	Able to get things done
Ethical	Beliefs about what is right and wrong
Logical	Clear, sound thinking, sensible and reasonable
Practical	Likely to succeed if tried, real not abstract
Precise	Exact, accurate, careful
Relevant	Closely connected to the topic or question
Reliable	Trustworthy, dependable
Significant	Important enough to be noticed or have an effect

Reproducible 2G
Student exploration: Can you identify an argument?

Arguments are ways in which we present our thinking to the world and convince others that our view is correct. Creating an argument is simply the way we reason or think though a question or problem.

Arguments have two main components: a belief followed by the reason we believe. Arguments are different than explanations, opinions or descriptions.

Consider the statements below and decide which ones are arguments. You may also notice that some arguments are stronger than others. Why do you think that is?

- Video games are not only for entertainment. They can also help kids develop social skills and build friendships.

- The school rule about not using cellphones in classrooms is outdated. I want it to change.

- I have soccer practice after school today. I will pack an extra snack so I have enough energy for the practice.

- The choices we make on how we travel to school affects climate change. We need to be environmentally responsible and walk to school.

- Youth have the power to make a positive influence in the world. This needs to begin with having opportunities in their schools and communities to make change.

- Students are getting bullied on social media. Students should not use social media until they are at least 16 years old.

- Stereotypes in the media have a negative impact on teens' body image. When teens see themselves represented in unrealistic sizes and shapes, they feel not good enough.

Student exploration: Errors in thinking and logic

Name: _____ Date: _____

Take a look at the following examples of errors in thinking and logic. Explain what seems "wrong" or "weak" about the thinking.

Statement	Thinking error analysis
He has been in trouble in the past, so he must have started the fight.	
She is so friendly and smart. She won't say no to helping me study.	
The reviews of the movie are bad, but my friend liked the movie. So I will like the movie.	
I learned how to skate from my brother. My brother is a good skater. So I am a good skater.	
I am older, therefore I know more than you.	
I will be really offended if you disagree with my idea.	
I have more "likes" than you so I must be more popular than you.	
He plays so many video games; he must have poor social skills.	
Go ahead, prove that I am wrong!	

Reproducible 21

A protocol for analysis of pedagogical documentation

Part 1: Studying the documentation

- Individually study the work of the learner.
- Make notes of what you see and hear to gather as much information as possible from the documentation:
  - What do you see?
  - What do you hear?

Part 2: Interpreting the documentation

- What does the documentation suggest about the learner's thinking?
- What are some questions we have?
- What are some assumptions we make about children and the learning?
- What ideas and questions are learners exploring?
- How did my words/actions influence the experience?
- Were there other influencing factors? What do I notice in different contexts?
- How might this information be used to plan for learning?

Part 3: Implications for practice

- What are the implications of this documentation for assessment for learning?
  - What further evidence of learning or information do you still need?
  - What might be the next action for the learner?
  - What does the evidence suggest to inform your pedagogical moves?

Adapted from: *http://www.edugains.ca/resourcesKIN/OtherResources/PLF/DesigningOpportunities/ProtocolforAnalysisofPedagogicalDocumention.pdf*

Teacher checklist: Purposeful planning for inquiry

Check which of the following statements represent how you plan for inquiry learning. Use this checklist for self-reflection, planning and sharing with colleagues, and to determine your next steps in deepening inquiry practice.

- I design learning tasks connected to essential questions in students' lives, subject disciplines and to the world, while focusing on clear and achievable learning targets.

- I design inquiry tasks that allow for optimal student autonomy and appropriate cognitive demand.

- I establish classroom conditions that support inquiry (e.g., purposeful student talk, individual reflective thinking, honouring student interests and experiences).

- My learning tasks and assessment plan detail inquiry learning opportunities based on the distinct stages of an inquiry process.

- My learning tasks and assessment plan promote growth in inquiry dispositions (e.g., curiosity, perseverance, risk-taking, open-mindedness).

- My learning tasks and assessment plan balance inquiry learning opportunities in addition to other learning opportunities.

- I have opportunities to co-plan, co-teach and co-assess inquiry learning activities and products with colleagues.

- I have resources that support my learning in inquiry-based pedagogies.

- Parents and community members will be apprised of and included in inquiry learning.

Student exploration: I see, I think, I wonder, I feel

Name: _____ Date: _____

Inquiry focus: _____

In each of the spaces record what you see, think, wonder and feel about your inquiry.

What do I see?

What do I think?

What do I wonder?

What do I feel?

Reproducible 3B
Questioning cube

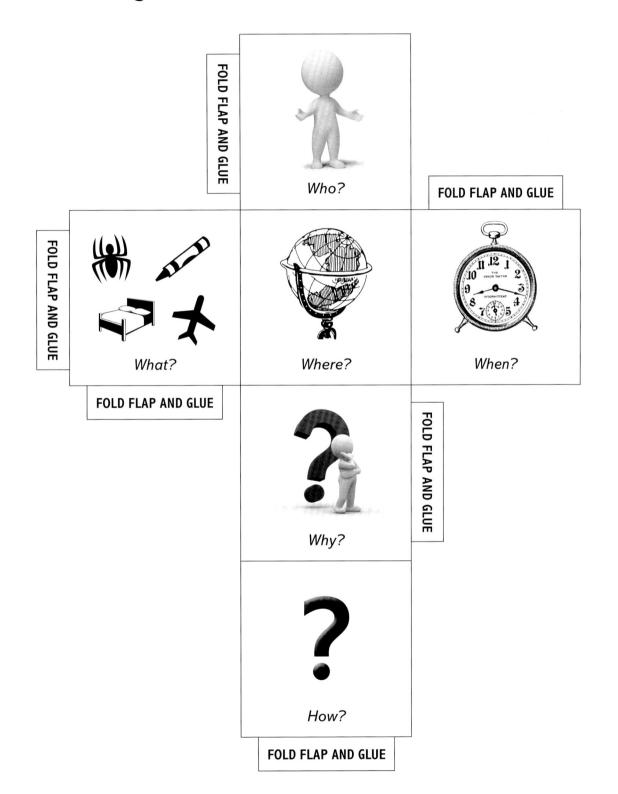

Reproducible 3C
Pick Two game cards

Set 1:

who 1	what 1
where 1	when 1
why 1	how 1

Set 2:

is/are 2	did/does 2
can/could 2	would/should 2
will 2	might 2

Student exploration: KWHLAQ chart

Name: _____   Date: _____

Key questions		My thinking
K	What do I **KNOW**?	
W	What do I **WANT** to know?	
H	**HOW** do I find out?	
L	What have I **LEARNED**?	
A	What **ACTION** will I take?	
Q	What **QUESTIONS** do I have?	

Reproducible 3E

Assessment planning template: Asks questions

Name: _____ Date: _____

Essential inquiry ability — Asking questions	Evidence gathered		
	Conversations	Observations	Products
Asks questions • Asks and refines relevant questions for different purposes (to get information, to clarify, to dispute, to drive an inquiry) and from different perspectives.			
Demonstrates curiosity • Actively asks many questions that demonstrate eagerness to learn. • Understands the importance of questioning to learning.			
(Gives and) Asks for reasons • Asks for justification of beliefs, proposals and solutions. • Thinks together. • Listens to, builds on, considers and assists with the questions of others. • Asks relevant questions of other people to further an inquiry (to get an opinion or some advice, to debate, to dispute, to inquire, to brainstorm).			
Understands what is currently known • Asks critical questions of "what is already known" (i.e., sources, data, strategies, theories).			
Puts it all together • Asks and understands the importance of analytical questions to improve their thinking at each stage of an inquiry.			

Inquiry rubric and self-check: Asks questions

Name: _____ Date: _____

Areas that need work	Standard for this criteria	How work exceeds expectations
	Asks questions • Asks and refines relevant questions for different purposes (to get information, to clarify, to dispute, to drive an inquiry) and from different perspectives.	
	Demonstrates curiosity • Actively asks questions that demonstrate eagerness to learn.	
	(Gives and) Asks for reasons • Asks for justification of beliefs, proposals and solutions.	
	Thinks together • Listens to, builds on, considers and assists with the questions of others. • Asks relevant questions of other people to further an inquiry (to get an opinion or some advice, to debate, to dispute, to inquire, to brainstorm).	
	Understands what is currently known • Asks critical questions of "what is already known" (i.e., sources, data, strategies, theories).	
	Puts it all together • Asks and understands the importance of analytical questions to improve their thinking at each stage of an inquiry.	

SOURCE: This single-point rubric is based on ideas from Jennifer Gonzalez's blog Brilliant or Insane: Education on the Edge, "Your Rubric is a Hot Mess; Here's How to Fix It."

Success criteria for a good question

Name: _____ Date: _____

☐ Is this something I am genuinely interested in and curious about?

☐ Is it open-ended (i.e., there's no right or wrong answer)?

☐ Will I have to think to answer this, not just find information?

☐ Can my question lead to more questions?

☐ Have I considered different ways to word my question?

- -

Success criteria for a good question

Name: _____ Date: _____

☐ Is this something I am genuinely interested in and curious about?

☐ Is it open-ended (i.e., there's no right or wrong answer)?

☐ Will I have to think to answer this, not just find information?

☐ Can my question lead to more questions?

☐ Have I considered different ways to word my question?

- -

Success criteria for a good question

Name: _____ Date: _____

☐ Is this something I am genuinely interested in and curious about?

☐ Is it open-ended (i.e., there's no right or wrong answer)?

☐ Will I have to think to answer this, not just find information?

☐ Can my question lead to more questions?

☐ Have I considered different ways to word my question?

Teacher checklist: Curiosity and questions in my classroom

Check which of the following statements represents your teaching practice. The focus of this checklist is questioning, an essential quality of inquiry thinking. Use this checklist for self-reflection, planning and sharing with colleagues, and to determine next steps in deepening inquiry practice.

- Students' questions are taken up in meaningful ways in my classroom.

- Students get to practise asking different types of questions in my classroom.

- Students understand why asking questions is important to learning in general, and inquiry learning in particular.

- Students in my classroom know there are different types of questions with different purposes and apply this knowledge.

- Students pose questions (including inquiry questions) and real world problems that relate to their lives and the "real world."

- Students ask analytical questions of their thinking during an inquiry.

- Students understand the criteria for effective questioning and can effectively self- and peer-assess questions.

- I use a variety of provocations to pique and sustain student curiosity, wonder and questioning.

- I pose questions and/or real world problems that relate to students' lives and the "real world."

- I pose questions and/or real world problems to provoke student curiosity and accelerate students' desire to learn.

- I organize factual knowledge around conceptual frameworks and open-ended inquiry questions to facilitate knowledge retrieval and application.

- I pose analytical questions to help students improve their thinking.

- I pose instructional questions to reveal students' prior knowledge, including preconceptions and misconceptions regarding important concepts.

- I assess students' questioning abilities through conversations, observations and products.

Brainstorming ways to gather evidence

Name: _____   Date: _____

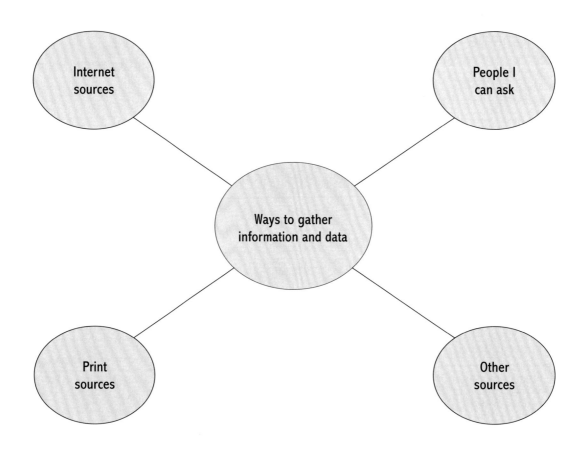

Assessing my point of view and assumptions

Name: _____ Date: _____

Inquiry: _____

My assumptions (what I already know or believe to be true)	
Where did I learn this?	
How might this impact my research?	
What are some possible different perspectives? Who might disagree with me?	

Evaluating sources and evidence: PASS

Name: _____ Date: _____

Inquiry focus: _____

Evidence being evaluated: _____

Key questions		My evaluation of the evidence
P	**PURPOSE** Why and when was it created? Is it important to my inquiry?	
A	**ACCURACY** Is the information correct, truthful and unbiased? Should I use it?	
S	**SOURCE** Who created it? Are they an expert? Are they believable?	
S	**SUPPORT** Is it supported by other information and sources? What does this tell me?	

Evaluating sources and evidence: USE IT

Name: _____ Date: _____

Inquiry focus: _____

Evidence being evaluated: _____

Key questions		My evaluation of the evidence
U	**USEFULNESS** How will it help me answer my question? How important is it?	
S	**SOURCE** Where did it come from? When was it created? Is it the original or has it been changed?	
E	**EVIDENCE** Is it supported by other evidence? What does it tell me?	
I	**IMPARTIAL** Is it fair and unbiased? Who created it? Why did they create it?	
T	**THINKING** Does it change my thinking? What does it tell me?	

Adapted from work developed by Jesse Denison and David Nolan during the York University certificate course in Inquiry-Based Learning (Spring 2015).

Evaluating evidence: SOURCE

Name: _____ Date: _____

Inquiry focus: _____

Evidence being evaluated: _____

Criteria	Question
Source	Where did it come from?
Objective	For what purpose was it created?
Usefulness	Is it relevant to the inquiry under investigation?
Reliability	Is it accurate, unbiased and reliable?
Context	Is it supported by other evidence?
Evidence	What does it prove?

Looking for bias in sources: FAN

Name: _____ Date: _____

Inquiry focus: _____

Stance	FOR	AGAINST	NEUTRAL
Source (title of book or website)			
Key points made			
Biases/missing voices			

RAN chart: Reading and analyzing nonfiction

Name: _____

Date: _____

What I think I know...	Yes, we were right!	Misconceptions	New information	Wonderings
	!	**X**	**★**	**?**

TLReT-Q Chart: Thinking, learning, rethinking

Name: _____ Date: _____

Inquiry focus: _____

Thinking	Learning	ReThinking
My initial thinking on this topic/problem:	My learning (the main sources I used, including print, media, or other people):	How I am rethinking this topic/problem:
Questions arising	Questions arising	Questions arising

Reproducible 4I

Assessing the investigating and exploring stage

Name: _____ Date: _____

Category	Criteria	Yes	Not yet
Knowledge and understanding	• Identifies available sources • Knows how different sources support the inquiry • Knows how to record sources		
Thinking	• Uses a variety of strategies to select credible, relevant information • Is thinking of ways to present the information		
Communication	• Shares ideas with peers electronically and in discussions • Records notes and sources • Shares thoughts and feelings about the inquiry process • Asks for help as needed		
Application	• Applies knowledge of how information is organized to help locate information • Makes connections between what is already known and new information		

Assessment planning template: Understands what is currently known

Name: _____   Date: _____

Essential inquiry ability — Understands what is currently known	Evidence gathered		
	Conversations	**Observations**	**Products**
Asks questions • Asks and refines relevant questions about the reliability, usefulness, authority and bias of evidence.			
Demonstrates curiosity • Actively asks many questions during the investigative stage. • Demonstrates an eagerness to explore, find things and learn.			
(Gives and) Asks for reasons • Asks for justification of a particular argument or position taken in a piece of evidence.			
Understands what is currently known • Has the necessary facts and information. • Is able to understand different perspectives within a body of evidence.			
Puts it all together • Understands when "enough" evidence has been collected and/or considered.			
Thinks together • Listens to, builds on, considers and assists others during the investigative process. • Asks relevant questions of other people to further an inquiry (gets an opinion or some advice, debates, disputes, inquires, brainstorms).			

Inquiry rubric and self-check: Understands what is currently known

Name: _____ Date: _____

Areas that need work	Standard for this criteria	How work exceeds expectations
	Asks questions • Asks and refines relevant questions about the reliability, usefulness, authority and bias of evidence.	
	Demonstrates curiosity • Actively asks many questions during the investigative stage. • Demonstrates an eagerness to explore, find things and learn.	
	(Gives and) Asks for reasons • Asks for justification of a particular argument or position taken in a piece of evidence.	
	Understands what is currently known • Has the necessary facts and information. • Is able to understand different perspectives within a body of evidence.	
	Puts it all together • Understands when "enough" evidence has been collected and/or considered.	
	Thinks together • Listens to, builds on, considers and assists others during the investigative process. • Asks relevant questions of other people to further an inquiry (gets an opinion or some advice, debates, disputes, inquires, brainstorms).	

This single-point rubric is based on ideas from Jennifer Gonzalez's Blog Brilliant or Insane: Education on the Edge, "Your Rubric is a Hot Mess; Here's How to Fix It."

Teacher checklist: Investigative mindset in my classroom

Check which of the following statements represents your current teaching practice. The focus of this checklist is on the investigative step of the inquiry process. You may want to use this checklist for self-reflection, for planning and sharing with colleagues, and to determine next steps in deepening inquiry practice.

- An investigative mindset is fostered in meaningful ways in my classroom.

- Conditions in my classroom encourage an investigative mindset.

- I purposefully plan our classroom experiences to minimize the impact of preconceptions and misconceptions.

- I locate age- and grade-appropriate resources for my students to drive their inquiry learning.

- I make sure that students are exposed to multiple perspectives during their inquiries.

- Students know that they cannot draw a conclusion before they have considered multiple perspectives.

- Students are learning how to determine the quality of sources.

- I know how to facilitate the investigative portion of an inquiry.

- I use a variety of provocations to pique and sustain student curiosity, wonder and questioning during the inquiry.

- I build in collaboration opportunities during the investigative phase of inquiry.

Student exploration: Making sense of my inquiry

Name: _____ Date: _____

Inquiry focus: _____

Question	My response
What do I think I might find?	
What did I find?	
What did I find that surprised me?	
What trends or patterns exist?	
Can I draw connections between ideas?	
What might have I overlooked?	
Did I gather evidence from the perspective of the people most impacted by the question/problem?	
What conclusion(s) can I draw from this evidence?	
Who is impacted by my conclusion and how are they impacted?	
What questions remain? What new questions do I have?	
How might I explore this further?	

PMI chart

Name: _____   Date: _____

Inquiry focus: _____

Use this template to help you draw a conclusion about the question you are investigating.

+

**Evidence that SUPPORTS
my conclusion**

**Evidence that DOES NOT
support my conclusion**

−

Other interesting evidence I uncovered

Reproducible 5C
Balance of evidence

Name: _____   Date: _____

Evidence for conclusion A	Evidence for conclusion B

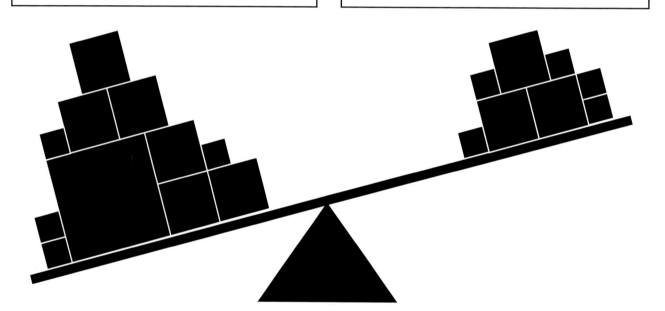

1. When drawing a conclusion, we shouldn't just look at the amount of evidence that supports one side or another of an inquiry; we should also examine the quality of evidence. Do you have some evidence you think is of better quality than other pieces of evidence? How much weight do you give to those pieces of evidence?

2. What about evidence that supports another conclusion? Does that mean you shouldn't consider the evidence? Or does it mean that your response to the inquiry question might be "There doesn't seem to be a definitive answer to the inquiry question..."

Reproducible 5D
Practicing synthesis

Name: _____ Date: _____

Task: Choose and/or create an inquiry question that interests your group.

Brainstorm your ideas in a group. Then complete the following steps:

1. Answer the questions as much as possible based on your ideas, beliefs and experiences.

2. Research some facts on the Internet related to the question.

3. Ask some other people to answer the question based on their experiences.

4. Combine the information from these three sources together. Write a short paragraph that combines all your information. Include paraphrase in your synthesis.

5. Have a peer assess your paragraph based on criteria for an effective synthesis.

6. Revise your paragraph.

7. Return to your group and create a collaborative paragraph that represents the best possible synthesis of all ideas gathered.

8. Share the paragraph with your class in an interesting way.

Possible questions to get you started:

*   If you could change one thing that happened in Canadian history, what would it be?

*   What is the best way to encourage recycling?

*   Should there be gender-neutral bathrooms in our school?

*   Should math (or coding) be a mandatory subject?

*   Are teenagers more creative than older people?

*   Does owning a pet make you calmer?

My question: _____

Making sense: Single-point rubric

Name: _____ Date: _____

Areas that need work	Success criteria for making sense	How work exceeds expectations
	Makes connections between sources	
	Makes connections between sources and what they already know	
	Paraphrases and summarizes sources	
	Makes valid inferences from sources	
	Demonstrates empathy	
	Generates new ideas	

Reproducible 5F

Assessment planning template: Puts it all together

Name: _____ Date: _____

Essential inquiry ability — Puts it all together	Evidence gathered		
	Conversations	Observations	Products
Asks questions • Asks and refines relevant questions about a body of evidence, inconsistencies in the evidence, and the weight of different pieces of evidence.			
Demonstrates curiosity • Actively asks many questions during synthesis and consolidation that demonstrate eagerness to learn.			
(Gives and) Asks for reasons • Asks for justification of evidence and gives reasons for a conclusion.			
Understands what is currently known • Is able to synthesize/consolidate "what is already known" (i.e., facts, data, theories).			
Puts it all together • Can synthesize a body of evidence into a coherent "whole." • Looks for patterns and trends in evidence. • Makes connections between ideas.			
Thinks together with empathy • Listens to, builds on, considers and assists others during the synthesis process. • Asks relevant questions of other people to further an inquiry (gets an opinion or some advice, debates, disputes, inquires, brainstorms).			

Inquiry rubric and self-check: Puts it all together

Name: _____   Date: _____

Areas that need work	Standard for this criteria	How work exceeds expectations
	Asks questions • Asks and refines relevant questions for different purposes (about a body of evidence, about inconsistencies in evidence, about the weight of different pieces of evidence) and from different perspectives.	
	Demonstrates curiosity • Actively asks many questions during synthesis and consolidation that demonstrate eagerness to learn.	
	(Gives and) Asks for reasons • Asks for justification of evidence and gives reasons for a conclusion.	
	Understands what is currently known • Is able to synthesize/consolidate "what is already known" (i.e., sources, data, strategies, theories).	
	Puts it all together • Can synthesize a body of evidence into a coherent "whole." • Looks for patterns and trends in evidence. • Makes connections between ideas.	
	Thinks together with empathy • Listens to, builds on, considers and assists others during the synthesis process. • Asks relevant questions of other people during the synthesis process (gets an opinion or some advice, debates, disputes, inquires, brainstorms).	

Teacher checklist: Synthesis and consolidation in my classroom

Check which of the following statements represents your current teaching practice. The focus of this checklist is on the consolidation step of the inquiry process. You may want to use this checklist for self-reflection, for planning and sharing with colleagues, and to determine next steps in deepening inquiry practice.

- Synthesis and consolidation skills are fostered in meaningful ways in my classroom.

- Conditions in my classroom encourage the development of synthesis and consolidation skills.

- I purposefully plan our classroom experiences to minimize the impact of thinking traps on the synthesis and consolidation phase of inquiry.

- I use age- and grade-appropriate templates to drive the inquiry learning of my students.

- I make sure that students have considered multiple perspectives while consolidating their evidence.

- Students know that not all evidence is of equal weight.

- Students are learning how to weigh both the amount and quality of evidence while drawing a conclusion.

- I know how to facilitate the synthesis portion of an inquiry.

- I use a variety of provocations to pique and sustain student curiosity, wonder and questioning during the synthesis phase of inquiry.

- I use a variety of methods to promote empathy in my students during the making sense stage (e.g., using drama, non-fiction, guest speakers and community members).

- I build in collaboration opportunities during the synthesis phase of inquiry.

Why reflecting is awesome!

Name: _____ Date: _____

Why reflecting
is awesome!

Criteria and advice for giving and receiving supportive critique

✓	Giving a critique
	I use assessment tools provided by the teacher to detail the quality of the work expected.
	I am positive and enthusiastic.
	I tell the person what is good and what is interesting.
	I ask for clarification if I am unsure about something.
	I am specific in my feedback.
	I don't give too many suggestions but focus on what is most important to improve the work.
	I don't change the person's work on their behalf (e.g., spelling, rewriting).

✓	Receiving and responding to a critique
	I listen carefully.
	I don't get defensive or angry.
	I respond to suggestions by explaining further.
	I show appreciation to the person for their critique.
	I take action on suggestions that I feel will most improve my work.
	I am prepared to explain why I rejected suggestions (if I do).

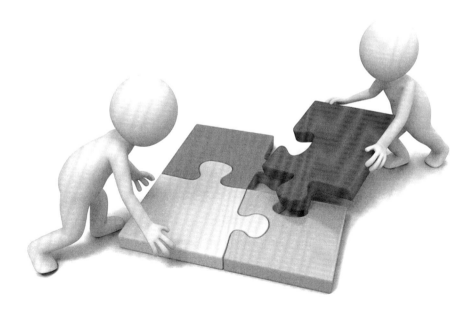

Image © Can Stock Photo / abluecup

Protocol for *providing* feedback:
Building on what's good

Critique buddy: _____   I am critiquing _____ 's work.

	Got it! (Record your evidence of success)	Not there yet
I listened attentively to my buddy's work.		
I provided supportive feedback. **GOOD JOB!**		
I provided specific suggestions for improvement. **CHANGE AHEAD**		
I will give new supportive feedback when we meet again. **NEW**		

Images © Can Stock Photo / nasir1164, © Can Stock Photo / Arcady, © Can Stock Photo / iqoncept, © Can Stock Photo / mejn

Protocol for *receiving* feedback:
Building on what's good

Inquiry learner: _____   My critique buddy is _____

	Got it! (Note your evidence of success)	Not there yet
I ask for feedback based on specific success criteria.		
I accept feedback.		
I use my buddy's feedback to change my work.		
I show my buddy how I used their feedback.		

Inquiry endpoint: Self-reflection

Name: _____ Date: _____

Self-reflection	My response
What stands out in your mind as you revisit your inquiry journey? (Consider how you thought and how you felt.)	
What have you learned about yourself as an inquiry learner? (Consider the skills and dispositions of an inquiry learner.)	
How might you apply your new learning at school and in your life?	
How could your teacher help you succeed the next time you do an inquiry?	

Images © Can Stock Photo / Denchik, © Can Stock Photo / michaeldb, © Can Stock Photo / coraMax, © Can Stock Photo / MasterofAll686

Reproducible 6F
Sharing your inquiry *process*: Planning sheet

Name: _____ Date: _____

I will share my inquiry process with the following people
(check any that apply):

☐ my peers   ☐ my family

☐ my teacher   ☐ community members

☐ other students/educators   ☐ a wider audience

Prepare to share the **highlights** of your inquiry process by including
answers to the questions in the following four categories. You may be asked
to share your answers from the four categories at different points in time.

How it all started . . .

• What were you curious about and why?

• What was your inquiry question/problem?

Where I went to next . . .

• Describe two sources that you chose to investigate and explain why.
  AND/OR

• What two strategies did you choose to create and innovate and why?

How I made sense of it all . . .

• How did you go about creating possible solutions, drawing
  conclusions, making new knowledge, and creating and innovating?

What this learning was like . . .

• Which parts of the process were easy, fun or interesting?

• Which parts of the process were challenging?

• What would you do differently next time?

• What questions remain about your inquiry topic?

• What product are you considering to communicate your
  inquiry learning?

Sharing your inquiry *product*: Planning sheet

Name: _____   My inquiry product is: _____

I will be sharing my inquiry product with . . . (check any that apply):

☐ my peers   ☐ my family

☐ my teacher   ☐ community members

☐ other students/educators   ☐ a wider audience

Why did you choose this product?

How does your product highlight important discoveries in your inquiry learning?

How does your product invite others to wonder about your question/problem?

Sources

Chapter 1

Barrow, L. "A brief history of inquiry – From Dewey to Standards." *Journal of Science Teacher Education*, 17, 2006, 265–78.

Berger, Warren. *A More Beautiful Question*. New York: Bloomsbury USA, 2014.

Boaler, J. *Experiencing school mathematics; Teaching styles, sex, and settings*. Buckingham, UK: Open University Press, 1997.

Brunner, Cornelia. "Inquiry-process model." Cited in "How to: Inquiry," YouthLearn, 2012. http://www.youthlearn.org/learning/planning/lesson-planning/how-inquiry.

Colyer, Jill and Jennifer Watt. *THINQ 4-6: Inquiry-based learning in the junior classroom*. Toronto: Wave Learning Solutions, 2016.

Friesen, Sharon and David Scott. "Inquiry-Based Learning: A Review of the Research Literature." June 2013. http://galileo.org/focus-on-inquiry-lit-review.pdf. Accessed on July 18, 2016.

Galileo Educational Network. "Dimensions of discipline based inquiry." http://inquiry.galileo.org/ch2/dimensions-of-discipline-based-inquiry/. Accessed on July 18, 2016.

McNeely, Clea and Jayne Blanchard. *The Teen Years Explained: A Guide to Healthy Adolescent Development*. Centre for Adolescent Health, John Hopkins Bloomberg School of Public Health, 2009.

Ontario Ministry of Education. *Learning for All: A Guide to Effective Assessment and Instruction for All Students, Kindergarten to Grade 12*. Toronto. Queen's Printer for Ontario, 2013.

Watt, Jennifer and Jill Colyer. *IQ: A Practical Guide to Inquiry-Based Learning*. Toronto: Oxford University Press, 2014.

Williams, D., Hemstreet, S., Liu, M., & Smith, V. "Examining how middle schools students use problem-based learning software." Proceedings of the EDMEDIA/ED-Telecom 98 World Conference on Educational Multimedia and Hypermedia, Frieburg, Germany, 1998. (ED 428 738).

All images courtesy the authors.

Chapter 2

Barron, Brigid and Linda Darling-Hammond. "Teaching for Meaningful Learning: A Review of Research on Inquiry-Based and Cooperative Learning." Excerpt from *Powerful Learning: What We Know About Teaching for Understanding*. San Francisco: John Wiley & Sons, 2008. http://files.eric.ed.gov/fulltext/ED539399.pdf. Accessed on July 18, 2016.

Colyer, Jill and Jennifer Watt. *THINQ 4-6: Inquiry-based learning in the junior classroom*. Toronto: Wave Learning Solutions, 2016.

Fullan, Michael and Maria Langworthy. *A Rich Seam: How New Pedagogies Find Deep Learning*. Pearson, 2014.

Harvard Graduate School of Education and National School Reform Faculty. "A Protocol for Analysis of Pedagogical Documentation." Adapted from *Making Learning Visible Project*. http://www.edugains.ca/resourcesKIN/OtherResources/PLF/DesigningOpportunities/ProtocolforAnalysisofPedagogicalDocumention.pdf. Accessed on July 18, 2016.

Ontario Ministry of Education. "Pedagogical Documentation Revisited" *Capacity Building Series K-12*. 2015. http://www.edu.gov.on.ca/eng/literacynumeracy/inspire/research/CBS_PedagogicalDocument.pdf. Accessed July 14, 2017.

Watt, Jennifer and Jill Colyer. *IQ: A Practical Guide to Inquiry-Based Learning*. Don Mills: Oxford University Press, 2014.

Wiggins, Grant. "Seven Keys to Effective Feedback." *Educational Leadership: Feedback for Learning*. 70(1), 2012, pp. 10–16.

Wiliam, Dylan. *Embedded Formative Assessment*. Bloomington IN, Solution Tree, 2011.

All images courtesy the authors.

Chapter 3

$150 Reward. [$150 reward cut of runaway slave Ranaway from the subscriber, on the night of the 2d instant, a negro man, who calls himself Henry May, ... William Burke, Bardstown, Ky., September 3d, 1838]. Bardstown, 1838. https://www.loc.gov/resource/rbpe.0220120b/

Barell, John. *Developing More Curious Minds*. Association for Supervision and Curriculum Development, 2003.

Berger, Warren. *A More Beautiful Question*. New York: Bloomsbury USA, 2014.

Christenbury, Leila and Patricia P. Kelly. *Questioning — A path to critical thinking*. ERIC Clearinghouse on Reading and Communication Skills, 1983.

Collins, Paul. *Harriet Tubman's Underground Railroad*. 1978 Copyright Paul Collins Art.

Fallen Feather Productions. "Kamloops Indian Residential School cattle truck children removed" (photograph). http://www.fallenfeatherproductions.com/photo_gallery.html. Accessed July 19, 2017.

Fortescue-Brickdale, Eleanor. *Arrival of the Brides (Filles du roi)*. 1871–1945. Courtesy of Library and Archives Canada, Acc. no 1996-371-1.

McTighe, Jay and Grant Wiggins. *Essential Questions: Opening doors to student understanding*. Association for Supervision and Curriculum Development, 2013.

Muth, Jon J. *The Three Questions*. Scholastic Press, 2005.

Parker, Lewis. *Expulsion of the Acadians from Prince Edward Island, 1758*. 1980-1982. Copyright Lewis Parker 2011.

Paul, Richard and Linda Elder. *The Miniature Guide to the Art of Asking Questions*. Tomales, CA: Foundation for Critical Thinking, 2010.

"Stowage of the British slave ship *Brookes* under the regulated slave trade act of 1788." c. 1788. Library of Congress Rare Book and Special Collections Division/LC-USZ62-44000. https://www.loc.gov/item/98504459/

Watt, Jennifer and Jill Colyer. *IQ: A Practical Guide to Inquiry-Based Learning*. Don Mills: Oxford University Press, 2014.

Chapter 4

Hoe, Ban Seng. "A Chinese work gang for the Great Northern Railway, circa 1909" in *Beyond the golden mountain: Chinese cultural traditions in Canada*. Hull, Quebec: Canadian Museum of Civilization, c1989.

Kuhlthau, Carol. *Seeking Meaning: A process approach to library and information services*. London: Libraries Unlimited, 2014.

Media Awareness Network and ERIN Research. *Young Canadians in a Wired World – Phase II*. 2005. http://www.erinresearch.com/documents/YCWW_II_survey_English.pdf. Accessed July 16, 2017.

Ontario Ministry of Education. *Adolescent literacy guide: A professional learning resource for literacy, Grades 7–12*. Toronto, 2012. http://www.edugains.ca/resourcesLIT/AdolescentLiteracy/Vision/AdolescentLiteracyGuide_Interactive.pdf. Accessed July 17, 2017.

Ontario School Library Association. *Together for Learning: School Libraries and the Emergence of the Learning Commons*. 2010. https://www.accessola.org/web/Documents/OLA/Divisions/OSLA/TogetherforLearning.pdf. Accessed July 16, 2017.

Rosenzweig, Roy. "Can History be Open Source? Wikipedia and the Future of the Past." *The Journal of American History*. Volume 93, Number 1, June 2006.

Wai-man, Lee (ed.). "Chinese railway workers' log camp beside railroad" in *Portraits of a challenge: an illustrated history of the Chinese Canadians*. Toronto: Council of Chinese Canadian in Ontario, 1984.

Chapter 5

Chiarotto, Lorraine. *Natural curiosity: A resource for teachers: Building children's understanding of the world through environmental inquiry*. Toronto: The Laboratory School at the Dr. Eric Jackman Institute of Child Study, Ontario Institute for Studies in Education, University of Toronto, 2011.

Krznaric, Roman. *Empathy: Why It Matters, and How to Get It*. TarcherPerigee, 2015.

Paul, Richard and Linda Elder. *Critical Thinking: Tools for taking charge of your learning and your life*. New York: Pearson, 2005.

"Synthesizing Information." *YouTube*, uploaded by GCFLearnFree.org, August 6, 2012, https://www.youtube.com/watch?v=7dEGoJdb6O0.

Chapter 6

Boud, David et al. (eds). *Reflection: Turning experience into learning*. London: Kogan Page, 1985.

Brookfield, Stephen D. *Becoming a Critically Reflective Teacher*. San Francisco: Jossey-Bass, 1995.

Costa, Arthur and Bena Kallick. *Learning and leading with habits of mind*. New York: ASCD, 2008.

Di Stefano, Giada, Francesca Gino, Gary Pisano and Bradley Staats. *Learning by thinking: How reflection improves performance*. Harvard Business School, 2014.

Marzano, Robert. *Becoming a Reflective Teacher*. Solution Tree, 2012.

National School Reform Faculty. "NSRF Protocols and Activities … from A to Z." www.nsrfharmony.org/free-resources/protocols/a-z. Accessed July 16, 2017.

Index

abilities
  determining current, 36–37
  essential, 26–29, 31, 32–33
assessment
  balanced, 38–39
  building partnerships, 33
  challenges of, 30
  communicating with parents, 45
  creation of plan, 139
  determining current abilities, 36–37
  documentation, 40–44
  essential abilities of learners, 26–29
  evaluations, 45–46
  and feedback, 33, 34–36
  gathering evidence, 38–42
  inquiry and curriculum, 30–31
  inquiry dispositions, 28–29
  and inquiry learning, 134
  and intermediate learners, 32–37
  interpreting evidence, 39
  of investigating and exploring, 95
  managing data, 42
  plans for, 46–47
  purpose, 26
  of questioning, 71–73
  responding to evidence, 39
  role of students, 135
  of synthesis activities, 109

bias
  in investigating and exploring,
    78–80
  student awareness of, 137

collaboration, 108–9, 128, 129, 141
communication
  with parents, 45
  vocabulary and inquiry thinking,
    141
concept maps, 101
critical thinking
  and inquiry dispositions, 8
  and inquiry learning stance, 27
  promoting, 10
  and reasoning, 28
critiquing, 125–27

curiosity
  and exploration, 22
  fostering, 6
  and inquiry dispositions, 8
  and inquiry learning, 27, 134
  promoting, 10
  relationship to learning, 135
  and technology, 6
curriculum
  assessing successful inquiry, 30
  and assessment, 30–31
  choosing target in, 139
  using, 31, 135

divergent thinking, 81
documentation, 40–42

emotions
  elicited by questions, 136
  and inquiry culture, 8
  of teachers using inquiry method, 17
empathy, 110–11, 138
evaluations, 45–46
exploring. *See* investigating and exploring

feedback, 33, 34–36
feelings and reflection, 119

Genius Hour, 16, 31, 68
graphic organizers, 66–67, 103

hopefulness
  and inquiry dispositions, 8
  and inquiry learning stance, 27, 98
  promoting, 10

inquiry
  aiding student to understand, 22
  appropriate resources, 140–41
  blended, 15–16
  and collaboration, 141
  Conversation cards, 22
  and empathy, 110–11, 138
  guided, 15–16, 139
  myths and misconceptions about, 18
  open, 15–16

reflection and sharing, 116–24
  sharing at end of, 123–24
  and student as learner, 22
  traits of, 11
inquiry assessment. *See* assessment
inquiry-based learning
  and intermediate learner, 20–21
inquiry dispositions
  and assessment, 29
  defined, 8
  features of classroom, 133
  and the inquiry learner, 29
  and inquiry stance, 27–28
  modelling by teacher, 9
inquiry learning. *See also* investigating
    and exploring
  advantages of, 4, 5
  and assessment, 134
  big ideas about, 132–38
  compared to other pedagogies, 3
  consolidation phase, 112
  continuum of, 134
  creating culture of, 8
  critiquing at end, 125–27
  and curiosity, 27, 134
  and curriculum, 135
  defined, 2
  history of, 4
  and hopefulness, 27, 98
  "making sense" stage, 98–99
  and need for high student
    engagement, 136
  and reasoning skills, 136
  role of student, 4, 7, 8
  role of teacher, 4, 15, 17, 89
  traits, 133
  types of, 5
  universality of, 7
  versions of, 11
inquiry models, 12, 13, 14
inquiry question, 135, 139
inquiry stance, 27, 137
inquiry teaching, 17
Internet
  credibility of sources on, 91–92
  search engines on, 86